I0074704

Heinous, Atrocious and Cruel

The Casebook of a Death Penalty Attorney

by

Terry Lenamon

With

Brooke Terpening

TELEMACHUS
PRESS

If you purchased this book without a cover you should be aware that this book is stolen property. It was reported as "unsold and destroyed" to the publisher and neither the author nor the publisher has received any payment for this "stripped book."

HEINOUS, ATROCIOUS AND CRUEL, THE CASEBOOK OF A DEATH PENALTY ATTORNEY

Copyright © 2011 by Terry Lenamon. All rights reserved, including the right to reproduce this book, or portions thereof, in any form. No part of this text may be reproduced, transmitted, downloaded, decompiled, reverse engineered, or stored in or introduced into any information storage and retrieval system, in any form or by any means, whether electronic or mechanical without the express written permission of the author. The scanning, uploading, and distribution of this book via the Internet or via any other means without the permission of the publisher is illegal and punishable by law. Please purchase only authorized electronic editions and do not participate in or encourage electronic piracy of copyrighted materials.

The publisher does not have any control over and does not assume any responsibility for author or third-party websites or their content.

Cover Designed by Brooke Terpening

Cover Art:
Copyright © iStockPhoto #1852350/Blue Lightening

Published by Telemachus Press, LLC
http://www.telemachuspress.com

ISBN # 978-1-937387-95-2 (eBook)
ISBN # 978-1-937387-96-9 (paperback)

Version 2011.12.03

Printed in the United States of America

10 9 8 7 6 5 4 3 2 1

Dedication

To my wife Gloria: the woman who finds the time and dedication to be a great mother and prosecutor, and balance the two;

To my loyal staff and friends, Brooke, Melissa, Andrea & Stuart and to my good friend Reba Kennedy;

And to my mom and dad who were always there for me, even when everyone else doubted:

Thank you.

Heinous, Atrocious and Cruel

The Casebook of a Death Penalty Attorney

Table of Contents

Foreword:
Death Really Is Different In Florida

AT THE OUTSET, death is different. At least the
Supreme Court thinks so. For those who are not lawyers, but
are interested in how a death penalty proceeding works in
Florida, read on. It will provide a good backdrop to the cases
in this book.

Florida has unique issues that make a death penalty proceeding even more challenging to an attorney than it already
is. We are one of the few states that will sentence a person to
death by a simple majority vote of the jury. A simple majority,
a single person, is all it takes for a recommendation of death.
It does not have to be unanimous. Once convicted, a lone
holdout on the jury is not enough to avoid a death sentence,
and even then, a judge may override a jury's decision for a life
sentence.

Florida has struggled to make its process Constitutional.
In *State v. Dixon*, 283 So. 2d 1 (Fla. 1973), the Supreme Court
of Florida upheld the constitutionality of the death penalty

statute. The court found that "death is unique punishment in its finality and in its total rejection of the possibility of rehabilitation."

However, not all murders are alike. The *Dixon* court confirmed that it was the intent of the legislature to reserve application of the death penalty "only to the most aggravated and least mitigated of the most serious crime." As a result, the Florida Legislature put into place a special process with safeguards so that the death penalty is applied properly after conviction of a capital crime.

Separate lawyers are required since capital trials consist of two separate phases, the guilt phase, and the penalty phase. The same jury that decides guilt in the first phase sits on the penalty phase to decide the punishment.

During penalty phase, the jury hears evidence concerning aggravators, circumstances that weigh toward death, and mitigators, those circumstances weighing in favor of mercy. The defense and prosecution can present new evidence supporting these circumstances. The jury then makes a sentencing recommendation based on these aggravators and mitigators.

The aggravating circumstances that can apply in any given first degree murder case are limited to those set forth in Florida Statute § 921.141(5). These circumstances are limited to fifteen possible aggravators:

1. § 921.141(5)(a): The capital felony was committed by a person previously convicted of a felony and under sentence of imprisonment or placed in community control or felony probation ("while serving a sentence").

2. § 921.141(5)(b): The defendant was previously convicted of another capital felony or of a felony involving the use or threat of violence to the person ("prior violent felony conviction").

3. § 921.141(5)(c): The defendant knowingly created a great risk of death to many persons ("great risk of death").

4. § 921.141(5)(d): The capital felony was committed while the defendant was engaged, or was an accomplice, in the commission of, or an attempt to commit, or flight after committing or attempting to commit, any robbery; sexual battery; aggravated child abuse; abuse of an elderly person or disabled adult resulting in great bodily harm, permanent disfigurement; arson; burglary; kidnapping; aircraft piracy; or unlawful throwing, placing, or discharging of a destructive device or bomb ("during course of a felony").

5. § 921.141(5)(e): The capital felony was committed for the purpose of avoiding or preventing a lawful arrest or affecting an escape from custody ("escape or avoiding arrest").

6. § 921.141(5)(f): The capital felony was committed for pecuniary gain ("pecuniary gain").

7. § 921.141(5)(g): The capital felony was committed to disrupt or hinder the lawful exercise of any governmental function or the enforcement of laws ("disrupting government function").

8. § 921.141(5)(h): The capital felony was especially heinous, atrocious, or cruel ("HAC").

9. § 921.141(5)(i): The capital felony was a homicide and was committed in cold, calculated and premeditated manner without any pretense of moral or legal justification ("CCP").

10. § 921.141(5)(j): The victim of the capital felony was a law enforcement officer engaged in the performance of his or her official duties ("LEO victim").

11. § 921.141(5)(k): The victim of the capital felony was an elected or appointed public official engaged in the performance of his or her official duties if the motive for the capital felony was related, in whole or in part, to the victim's official capacity ("government official performing duties").

12. § 921.141(5)(l): The victim of the capital felony was a person less than 12 years of age ("child under 12").

13. § 921.141(5)(m): The victim of the capital felony was particularly vulnerable due to advanced age or disability, or because the defendant stood in a position of familial or custodial authority over the victim ("advanced age or disability").

14. § 921.141(5)(n): The capital felony was committed by a criminal street gang member, as defined in § 874.03 ("street gang member").

15. § 921.141(5)(o): The capital felony was committed by a person designated as a sexual predator pursuant to § 775.21 or a person previously designated as a sexual predator who had the sexual predator designation removed ("sexual predator").

The mitigating circumstances that can apply in any given first degree murder case are identified in Florida Statute § 921.141(6). Unlike the aggravators, the eighth mitigator is extremely open-ended. Almost any extenuating circumstance in the client's life is allowed. The eight mitigators are:

1. § 921.141(6)(a): The defendant has no significant history of prior criminal history.

2. § 921.141(6)(b): The capital felony was committed while the defendant was under influence of extreme mental or emotional disturbance.

3. § 921.141(6)(c): The victim was a participant in the defendant's conduct or consented to the act.

4. § 921.141(6)(d): The defendant was an accomplice in the capital felony committed by another person and his participation was relatively minor.

5. § 921.141(6)(e): The defendant acted under extreme duress or under the substantial domination of another person.

6. § 921.141(6)(f): The capacity of the defendant to appreciate the criminality of his conduct or to conform his conduct to the requirements of law were substantially impaired.

7. § 921.141(6)(g): The age of the defendant at the time of the crime.

8. § 921.141(6)(h): The existence of any other factors in the defendant's background that would mitigate against imposition of a death sentence.

The trial judge performs the next step by actually determining the sentence. Although the trial judge gives great weight to the jury recommendation, the trial judge is not bound by the jury's recommendation. The rationale is that a trial judge has more experience in both the criminal process and facts of crimes. What the average person, inexperienced in crimes, thinks is incredibly significant or especially heinous, may not in balance be so significant or heinous. The cool reason of a judge also serves to counterbalance any overly inflammatory prosecution.

The trial judge's last step is justification of a death sentence in writing. This step is necessary so that the sentence is open to judicial review. Judicial review ensures that the issue of life or death was decided according to the rule of law.

There is one final safeguard in place. The Supreme Court of Florida must review all death sentences. The court reviews the sentence for proportionality to ensure that the application is not unreasonable or inappropriate when compared to other cases. Thus, the defendant has one last opportunity before a court of law to argue against the most severe and final of all punishments.

The importance of mitigation in this process cannot be overstated. The results of a thorough mitigation investigation are very effective in persuading a jury to vote for life instead of death at the end of penalty phase. Often the mitigation is presented to prosecutors before trial begins as a waiver package to convince the state not to seek the death penalty.

Mitigation is so important in capital cases that the American Bar Association ("ABA") has issued "The ABA Guidelines for the Appointment and Performance of Counsel in Death Penalty Cases (2003)." The ABA Guidelines requires that each capital defense team have at least one mitigation specialist.

The role of the mitigation specialist on a death penalty case is broad. A mitigation specialist must develop an in-depth and comprehensive social history of the client. This requires identification, location, and retrieval of all records regarding the client, as well as the records of all immediate and extended family members. In addition to obtaining records, the mitigation specialist must conduct comprehensive interviews with the client and as many individuals as possible who have known the client.

Locating and interviewing witnesses in a capital case, especially family members, is more difficult than it would seem. It is a sensitive endeavor, requiring exceptional time, patience, and skill. One reason is that family members, like the client, may also suffer from mental retardation, mental illness, and substance abuse.

In addition, obtaining the trust of the witnesses is a key issue. Family members in particular are suspicious of talking to anyone about the client. They often assume that the reason for the interview is to incarcerate or hurt their loved one. Others are naturally reluctant to reveal painful and embarrassing facts regarding family history to a stranger. Consequently, a significant amount of time must be spent in overcoming various impairments, but also in demonstrating a sincere commitment to assisting the client. These difficulties, combined with the length of time between childhood and the time of the offense or post-conviction investigation, often requires that witnesses be re-interviewed to obtain valid, reliable data.

The mitigation specialist should verify the information by obtaining corroboration from more than one source. For example, a head injury and its effects should be documented by interviewing anyone who witnessed the injury or knew the client before and after the trauma as well as the treating medical professional. Additionally, all medical records must be obtained. This is essential so that a medical, psychological, or neurological expert can draw accurate conclusions about the effects of the injury on the client's perception, judgment, and behavior.

The penalty phase attorney must begin work on the case as early as possible in the preparation of mitigation. Mitigation investigations routinely require between 200 and 500 hours of uninterrupted intensive work over a period of six months to two years, depending on the complexity of the case, accessibility of family members and other witnesses, the nature and extent of the impairment of the client, and the availability of expert witnesses. A competent mitigation investigation is a critical part of the defense of a capital crime. Without adequate time and resources for thorough mitigation, the defense is seriously compromised.

This is an abbreviated description of the process. Volumes have been written on Florida's death penalty system. Each year the Public Defender's Office holds an excellent intensive multi-day seminar on capital defense. I have listed other good sources to explore for those with a deeper interest.

Brooke Terpening

Introduction

I HAVE BEEN practicing criminal law for a long time, and for many years, my focus has been on defending individuals that face a sentence of death in Florida capital murder trials. Not a week goes by where someone does not ask me how I can do this work, and why I do what I do.

Why *do* I defend what some call "the worst of the worst"? Just why is it that I defend those people that have been described on more than one occasion (and by more than one prosecutor) as the worst of our society?

In Florida, where I live and do most of my work, death penalty cases have two lawyers, known as first chair and second chair. As first chair in a death penalty case, my job is concerned with the guilt finding of the defendant. As second chair, my job is to convince the jury to spare the life of the person if they are convicted. This job is known as "mitigation," a dedicated area that I practice within, focusing upon the mental health aspects of homicide defendants.

"How can you represent those people?"

There are all the usual stock answers. "I am defending the Constitution." "The death penalty is not a cost-effective solution." "There is no deterrent value." "As for retribution, is a life in a cage worse than death?" "The system is not perfect, and innocent people have been sentenced to death." "Death row is overwhelmingly populated by the poor and disadvantaged."

And all of these answers are true, but they don't tell you the whole story.

Fundamentally, I do this because I want to understand. Why did this happen? How did this person arrive at my figurative doorstep, accused of a horrendous crime? What are the factors, the background, the events that led this person here?

Every person has a story. There is always some underlying common humanity in even those convicted of the most brutal crimes. It is my job to bring these mitigating factors to the jury, to shed light on the darkest heart and most disturbed mind.

And I'm bringing you this selection of cases from my briefcase — war stories, if you will, that I think exemplify the work that I do, because I think that you may share the same core need that I have — the need to know WHY.

Chapter One:
Mentally Ill

KATHERINE HAD SUCH a sweet face, even in death. I was sad, really sad, looking at the police file photographs of this pretty little toddler. Her life had been taken from her by her mother, the woman supposed to protect her. At eighteen months old, what did little Katherine know as her mommy was placing her underneath the water. Was she scared? Was she trusting?

Eighteen months old. I reflected on the pain that Katherine must have experienced. Such a horror, but a horror not that different than many of the other cases I'd come across in my job as a death penalty defense lawyer. I'd see even worse in the years to come.

I put the photos back into the manila envelope, and put that into the file folder. Katherine's mother was my new client, Yvette Yallico. My client: another child.

Yvette was eighteen years old at the time she was arrested for killing her daughter. A young woman with a significant history of mental illness, Yvette herself was born to a teen mother who had been physically and sexually abused. The cycle of violence and destruction that began its evolution with Yvette's mother I would later learn continued with Yvette herself.

At the time of Katherine's homicide, Yvette was still a child: a high school senior getting ready to take her high school competency evaluation test. Married at 16 years old to a 28-year-old man, Yvette had wandered into the same world that her mother experienced when she had married at age 13.

Yvette's young mother had used drugs during Yvette's pregnancy, had been sexually assaulted during her pregnancy, and ultimately diagnosed with gonorrhea at Yvette's birth. Yvette's dad? Yvette never knew her father. Her mother was not sure who the father was, acknowledging that she had multiple sexual partners during the period of time that she had become pregnant with Yvette.

The first time I came face to face with Yvette Yallico was in a Miami jail cell shortly after I was appointed to the case because of a Public Defender conflict. Yvette was housed at the Women's detention center in Miami. The detention center has a large open space for prisoners to meet with family. Attorneys could find privacy with their clients if they were lucky enough to get one of three miniscule conference rooms bordering the large room. I was lucky and appropriated one of the rooms before handing a pink inmate request slip to the guards.

I was surprised at how young the woman seemed that was brought to the attorney's room by guards. Yvette was barely five feet tall and slightly overweight, with a very pretty face and dark eyes. She seemed very out of touch with her surroundings, and when I informed her that I was taking over her case, she had no response. It was surreal because in the hour that I spoke to her, she kept expressing her desire to get out of prison so she could take her finals.

I wasn't her first lawyer. Many times, public defenders have to conflict (ask the court for another lawyer to be appointed to the case) because people who may be witnesses in the new case are, or have been, involved in other pending or past cases of the Public Defender's Office. Lawyers can't muddy the waters between cases.

When the case prosecuting Katherine's death arrived, the public defender's caseload soon made it apparent on the surface that their representation of the defendant in this new matter, Yvette, would be a conflict of interest with cases they'd already undertaken. It wouldn't be fair or ethical for the public defender to do otherwise than to ask that an outside attorney be appointed to take over the defense. So, that's how I got involved with the defense of Yvette Yallico.

Back in 1999, there was only a small group of lawyers in private practice who were being appointed to death penalty cases in Florida. I was one of those. We were called death-qualified.

I still remember getting the phone call from Pat Nally, a public defender friend of mine. Pat had been assigned to represent Yvette and he had already spent a great deal of effort in a very short time frame working up the case before the conflict was discovered.

"Terry, can you take this one? It's bad — there's a baby who's the victim — and it's short notice." We discussed scheduling, ruled out conflicts on my end, things like that. Would I take a case where a baby had died? Yes, I would. That's my job. It's what I'm supposed to do.

Soon, the court order was in place, substituting me as attorney in charge for Yvette Yallico. Now I was the appointed attorney to represent this indigent citizen in a case where the state of Florida would seek her death as its penalty for a crime.

Reviewing the Files

First things first, I reviewed the files — the public records as well as the defense work done thus far. I discovered that the Miami-Dade Public Defender's Office had done its typical impeccable job in representing this woman early on in the case. Having served as a public defender in Miami for a number of years before entering in private practice, I had learned the importance of "leaving no stone unturned" in the representation of a capital defendant. I was first introduced to this concept through the work of some great lawyers who worked in that office and who treated every death penalty case as if it were the most important case on the docket. This was no different. They'd done their job.

From the public defender's file, I learned that the Miami public defender became involved in this case after teen mom Yvette Yallico had been interrogated and then arrested by the police for murdering her child and brought before a magistrate judge at First Appearance. Interesting gap. Immediately upon appointment by the judge as Yvette's indigent defense counsel, I began going through the paperwork. The Public

Defender's file showed that they had started to corral resources to make sure that the investigation in this case was done properly and expeditiously. Good. Every resource we could muster would be needed. Yvette remained in jail as I came up to speed.

The First Mental Health Investigation After the Crime

It was readily apparent from the get-go that Yvette Yallico was suffering from some kind of massive mental health issue, some sort of traumatic breakdown. No one on either side of the case disputed that Yvette acted strangely.

Typically, in these cases, the lawyer wants to get an evaluation done as closely as possible to the time of arrest. In the perfect world, obviously, you would want the police initially to have her evaluated by an independent, neutral psychologist or psychiatrist. However, we don't live in the perfect world and sometimes things aren't always the way they are supposed to be. From the files, I discovered that Yvette was first evaluated by Mary Haber, a well-known forensic psychologist with a history of experience and a dynamic personality to go along with it.

Dr. Haber had met with Yvette Yallico and had formed an opinion. Dr. Haber's information had been provided to the public defender's office, and now it had passed to me when I took over the case. More on Dr. Haber later.

After my initial conversation with Pat, before I ever laid eyes on Yvette Yallico or saw all the records, it was clear to me that this was a mental health defense case: insanity was probably going to play a role in the defense of this teenager.

Psychological opinions like this first one by Dr. Haber would be critical to the case. Little did I know at that point how horrific and extensive Yvette Yallico's mental illness would prove to be.

Psychiatric Issues Since Age 11

Psychologically, the journey for Yvette that ended in her arrest in October 1999 began many years before. Yvette began to experience psychotic episodes as early as age 11. The teachers and school counselors took note, and eventually Yvette was categorized as a severely emotionally disturbed child within the Miami-Dade public school system. I learned from her school records that Yvette had been evaluated many times resulting in multiple diagnoses including psychosis, NOS ("not otherwise specified"), schizophrenia, and bipolar disorder.

Psychology is never a perfect science, of course. Different doctors evaluating the same individual can reach different conclusions. In this case all of Yvette's hospitalizations — beginning with an initial hospitalization at age 11 to her final hospitalization before the arrest, which occurred about 6 months prior to Katherine's death — were all related to acute psychotic episodes, which included a pattern of hallucinations and delusions. Bizarre behaviors that had all been recorded in various files now became a part of my defense preparation.

These documented episodes included Yvette believing that she had the ability to talk to Jesus, and that Jesus had told her to eat only bread. Sometimes, Yvette referred to herself as Yahweh. On other occasions she reported that God, or Yahweh, was constantly speaking to her. According to Yvette, God told her that marijuana was natural and good, and God had given her suicidal thoughts. If she committed suicide, she would show her devotion to him. Yvette also believed at times that the devil was inside of her. Routinely, she heard voices and "received" special messages from the television. Many of the delusions and hallucinations were followed by a series of manic sleepless nights, odd behavior, and even some promiscuity. There was clearly a longstanding pattern of abnormality.

An Abnormal Crime Scene
The story of this tragedy began one sunny afternoon in October 1999, when Miami police logged an emergency call from an adult male requesting paramedics go to his North Miami apartment because he had just received a call from his wife Yvette telling him that there had been an accident involving their child.

The father, Juan, told police that his wife Yvette had just called him at work to say their baby had drowned. Unable to get a clear answer from Yvette as to what had happened, he was calling the cops for help. In a panic, he also called his mother.

Witness interviews revealed that Juan's mother arrived at the couple's apartment at the same time as Juan. Upon arrival, Juan ran up to the second floor apartment and went in — only to find his baby girl Katherine submerged underwater in the bathtub, floating face up, with no response. Not moving. Not breathing.

A neighbor showed up to help. Yvette stood nearby, unemotional and detached, while Juan and the neighbor tried to resuscitate the baby. The police arrived with paramedics, who transported the baby to the hospital. Katherine was DOA.

At the apartment, law enforcement began their investigation. Yvette remained on the scene. She had not asked to go in the ambulance, and now she was questioned by the police. The officers noticed straightaway that the young mother was showing a detachment: there was no emotion here, no concern about her child. After questioning her for a short period, they placed Yvette in the back seat of a police vehicle to discuss the matter in more detail. What had happened to her baby that day?

During that squad car chat, their notes described Yvette as being more interested in finding out when she would be done with the questioning so she could get back to studying for her high school competency exam than knowing anything about Katherine. Suspicion rose about Yvette.

Police transported her down to the Miami police station in that squad car, and questioning continued at the station. Yvette told them what had happened.

Conflicting Statements

In the first two statements, she described the drowning as an accident. Yvette told the police that she was cooking dinner and had left the baby playing in the bathtub alone, and Katherine had drowned. It was an accident, she explained.

Yvette went into the bathroom and found the baby floating, and she called her husband.

However, at the police station Yvette was observed joking with several officers, flipping through her yearbook of the high school she was attending (the cops had provided it), and not acting like a mother whose child has just died. Yvette was clearly detached from the situation, and she was not concerned about her child. Not once during that initial stay at the police station did she ever ask to speak to Katherine or to see her baby.

Law enforcement deliberated. Ultimately, it was decided that Yvette would be charged with manslaughter, which is a negligence-related crime. Yvette was moved to a waiting area, where she would then be transported to the jail. And here is where I discovered a key event in the case took place, there in that window of time between the questioning and the jail transport.

Sitting there, waiting for her ride, Yvette was questioned yet again by an experienced homicide sergeant. His was the third police interview that afternoon after Katherine's death. He interviewed the teenager there, alone. Him and her.

With just the two of them talking, the homicide cop brought up to Yvette that it must have been hard being a single parent; tough to be a young mom; yadda yadda yadda. From a spin calculated to evoke sympathy, something this pro was trained to do, sure enough he was able to obtain a confession. Yvette admitted to drowning the child because of all the stress that she had suffered during the preceding weeks. It wasn't an accident. Oh, and he had come prepared: this third conversation was tape recorded.

By the time her ride showed up and Yvette was transported to the Miami-Dade County jail. The charge had
changed to first degree murder. Now, the death penalty was
on the table.

The First 72 Hours

After her arrest, the public defender brought in a forensic
social worker to document both her behavior and note significant conversations that would be ultimately used in her
defense when raising insanity. This was savvy of them to do,
and it would prove invaluable to my defense.

I appreciated the hard work of Pat Nally here. Corrections usually isn't that cooperative in making sure that our
clients are immediately accessible, no matter how important a
defense lawyer thinks that this may be. Simply put, our emergency isn't theirs. Although Miami-Dade Corrections is one
of the few locations you can see your client pretty much at
any time, Pat Nally had jumped this facility hurdle to get a
forensic social worker in to see Yvette. He also overcame
resource and budget hurdles to get the Yallico investigation
moving quickly. Good work and a relief to me as I began the
job of defending Yvette. Without Pat's efforts, there would
not have been an experienced forensic social worker hired
and at work quickly, able to document and evaluate, write a
report, have notes, and ultimately become a witness in the
case in favor of the defendant.

Forensic social workers are vital to cases like Yvette's.
Lawyers are not normally trained to deal with mental health
issues, or issues relating to emotional or traumatic events that

our clients often face. Smart lawyers know the limitations of
their expertise, and get the outside help they need for their
case.

It is especially important to build an expert team when
you're an attorney dealing with a homicide case. Yvette's case,
like most where mental health is being addressed, needed that
expert touch as soon as possible — and within a critical window that I believe is the first 72 hours after the defendant's
arrest. For Yvette especially, one defense key was her state of
mind at the time of the crime.

The Nally files revealed that a forensic social worker had
indeed met with Yvette Yallico during that time window.
Elisa Crudo had documented both her observations of Yvette
as well as the history Yvette had provided and Yvette's
responses to certain questions — which ultimately would be
supportive of proving Yvette's state of mind at the time of
Katherine's death. And, the file showed that drugs were being
given to Yvette down at the jail. Serious drugs.

The truth was that Yvette was never reality-based, even
where she was being heavily medicated to the utmost with
numerous types of drugs. Sitting in jail, her baby dead, Yvette
would constantly talk about graduating high school, and how
important it was for her to finish her test. When would they
let her out to take the test? She wanted to go to homecoming,
she was a senior — it was a big deal for seniors to go to
homecoming. All of this behavior was recorded in our forensic files.

Building the team, I saw the continuing need not only
for a forensic social worker but also a guilt phase investigator,
and Frank Miranda joined the Yallico defense team. (Frank is

now a mitigation specialist.) While Elisa Crudo had done an excellent job interviewing Yvette, she was with the public defender's office, so I hired my own forensic social worker.

These two people took on roles that were critical to my job. Not only did I not have the experience and knowledge to do this kind of interview and work, it was important to have professionals with savvy in dealing with young people like my teen mom client. In addition, I was lucky enough to get Odalis Acosta, a former public defender social worker who I had met some years ago, to join the team, and she hit the ground running.

The Jail Records

In a case like Yvette's, where a jailed defendant is psychotic or suffering from mental illness, many times the correction officers catch on quickly to the special circumstances. Within a very short period after they get responsibility for the individual (and this can be hours, not days), the jailers will begin dispensing drugs to the inmate. Oftentimes these are seriously strong, anti-psychotic drugs.

Sure enough, Yvette's file showed that she was being given serious anti-psychotics by the corrections officers shortly after she was admitted to the Miami-Dade facility. This was an important fact for the defense, because an individual's perception, her state of mind, her appearance, and her overall tenure becomes different over time than at the time of the event. The records told us these professionals thought Yvette needed these drugs at the jail and that Yvette appeared to need anti-psychotic medication after she had been questioned at the scene and at the police station. There she had given three different statements.

Mounting the Defense

After reading all the records, I became clear that Yvette Yallico was psychotic when she drowned her child. Insane. My job as a lawyer was to turn this fact into a legal defense, and protect her from the death penalty that the prosecution was seeking. Now, the issues with insanity are always complicated because defendants don't always admit to what they have done. Understandable.

In Yvette's case, for example, the first two statements she gave to the police denied any involvement in the killing. It was in the third statement that she confessed to the drowning.

It became the defense team's job to gain the confidence of Yvette, so that she saw that we cared for her and that we were there to help her in every way possible. Our hope was that she would disclose to us what really happened once she trusted that we did have compassion and empathy for her plight. This bond of trust would be critical to her defense.

I continued to build the defense team that Pat Nally had begun. I put investigators on the job of finding out everything they could about this teenager's short history. We discovered that six months before the drowning, Yvette was delusional. After claiming that two men had raped her, she had been "Baker-Acted" (involuntarily institutionalized) at Jackson Memorial Hospital where she was diagnosed with schizophrenia chronic paranoid type. Her husband checked her out of Jackson against medical advice two weeks after she was admitted. We would need to know why he had done so. Investigation discoveries found that Yvette had attended several emotionally handicapped programs, and we got even more documentation of her history as a SED student (Severely Emotionally Disordered) in the Miami-Dade school system, including a laundry list of psychological labels that had been placed on Yvette since she was around ten years old. Team investigators found out that Yvette was routinely teased by kids at school, who called her "psycho," and that during her pregnancy she had made numerous comments at school about not being ready to have the child.

Full police files obtained during our investigation also contained significant observations that the police and jailers had placed in their paperwork (which would be fleshed out in their depositions), providing even more facts supporting Yvette's insanity. Cops had noted her inappropriate laughter at the police station, her rambling about her family dancing like dead people, her thoughts about dressing up in all white and believing she was an angel. Two of these police recollections particularly stand out in my memory today. One was strange behavior at the station: Yvette singing the "Kit Kat" candy bar jingle while she was walking into the police elevator on her way to jail. The other, the saddest one: one police officer noted that post-arrest, Yvette explained that Katherine would be coming back to her after Yvette had prayed to God.

We had to have an expert to testify on the mental health issues, someone with the credentials to take all these facts along with evaluation and tell the jury what was going on with Yvette Yallico. It was decided after some significant discussion among the team that a doctor who was experienced in schizophrenia and bipolar disorder, and who had a significant experience in diagnosing psychotic disorders, was needed. We found our guy in New York City.

Hiring Dr. Xavier Amador

The importance of Dr. Xavier Amador joining the defense team cannot be underestimated. While Dr. Mary Haber is a forensic psychologist who is an excellent advocate, she was also from the local area and came with baggage the state would use against us, since she had already appeared as an expert in several of my past cases. I knew in advance that Mary Haber would be labeled my "hired gun," suggesting that her opinion would be biased toward the defense.

Yvette's defense needed an independent expert who could interact more distinctly with the state attorney in my presentation in the hopes of resolving the case as well as testifying to the jury at trial. I got on the phone and asked people I respected who they could recommend. I learned of Dr. Xavier Amador from Steve Harper, a well-respected mitigation lawyer who worked at the Public Defender's office.

Dr. Xavier Amador, from Columbia University's Department of Psychology, agreed to participate in Yvette's evaluation to determine whether she was insane at the time of Katherine's death. We were lucky to get him, given our budget constraints and his level of expertise. Expert fees for indigent defense, after all, would be paid by the state — not our client or her family.

At first, Dr. Amador was a little bit reluctant to get involved in a case in Miami, considering that he was in New York City, but after some persuasion and discussions about Mrs. Yallico and the finality involved in a death case — Yvette's life was on the line here — he became more receptive and ultimately agreed to become involved. It turned out that Yvette's case hit close to home: Dr. Amador understood first-hand the ravages of severe mental illness since his own brother is a diagnosed schizophrenic. Dr. Amador had written a memoir of living with his mentally-challenged brother, as well as his brother's life with schizophrenia, and how this led Dr. Amador into his chosen field. Reading his book, I knew that Dr. Amador was the man for our team — but learning of his past criminal defense affiliations really nailed it. Dr. Amador had participated in a number of high profile cases, including the Unabomber case, where the death penalty was avoided, in part due to Dr. Amador's opinion regarding Ted Kaczynski's mental illness and, particularly, agnosia. Part of agnosia involves the inability of its victim to understand that they are suffering from mental illness, so Dr. Amador also helped the defense team in getting Ted Kaczynski to agree to a plea agreement involving a life sentence.

Dr. Xavier Amador was exactly the psychological expert we needed. He understood the psychological challenges we faced, and he was savvy about the legal machinery involved in a death case. It was a satisfying day when we retained Dr. Amador to help on the Yallico defense.

Dr. Xavier Amador's Evaluation of Yvette

Dr. Amador learned during his interviews with Yvette that, after she was brought home from Jackson by her husband, she began getting messages that she was supposed to drown her child. There were several of these messages.

The first message appeared to Yvette while she was watching *"The Joy Luck Club,"* a movie where a woman who has problems with her child drowns the baby. The movie, Yvette explained, had given her messages to drown her baby, too.

Other messages began to arrive: songs on the radio or TV told Yvette to drown the baby. On the day of the homicide, moments before it happened, Yvette had another message to drown the baby. During her impulse to do so, Yvette told Dr. Amador that the shampoo and soap were telling her not to drown the baby. Yvette admitted understanding that she needed to take her pills when she was receiving these messages, but she didn't take the pills. She had not been taking her medications. Yvette admitted to Dr. Amador that she followed the messages, and drowned Katherine by holding the child underneath the water until she stopped moving.

Getting Ready to Defend Yvette Yallico in Court

Preparation for trial always involves two things: facts and law. From the beginning, it was clear that insanity was going to be the only defense available to us. Not an easy legal task, even with the plethora of mental illness substantiation that we had gathered.

Historically, proving insanity has been an uphill battle in criminal courts. After President Reagan was shot, there was a national outcry to change the legal standards for a mental health defense and as a result, in Florida the *McNaughton Rule*

is applied to any insanity case. Harder burden for us. Under
McNaughton, a person cannot know right from wrong. The
classic example lawyers hear in law school is that the person
must think they were slicing up a watermelon, not a human
being. Yvette was severely mentally ill when she killed
Katherine, but could we prove the legal defense of insanity in
a court of law?

The state's theory, of course, was that Yvette was not
legally insane. They would argue that she was unhappy in her
marriage and unhappy with the child, never wanted the child,
was involved in sexual promiscuity, and having multiple
affairs on the marriage. She killed her baby because she
thought it was expedient to do so, so she could be free to
have fun.

How to fight the prosecution's stance? First, we had the
many bizarre statements that Yvette had made to many people in the weeks and months presiding the killing. Lots of
witnesses' names were added to our witness list.

Second, to prove legal insanity, we studied the legal
implications of Mrs. Yallico's diagnosis. Medicine and law
don't jive here, never have: legal insanity is a much narrower
concept than psychological insanity. With every detail in the
fact pattern, the defense team would have to build an argument that everything the state submitted as supportive of
their theory of premeditated first degree murder were facts
that were easily explained and understandable in light of the
significant mental health issues of Yvette.

Working Two Fronts

You always work two fronts in a case like this. Without breaking stride, you prepare for a courtroom battle while simultaneously seeking the possibility of resolution outside of trial. Early on in the case, as my team was working hard on getting ready for trial, I began working toward negotiating a resolution outside the courtroom.

First, who would I be dealing with from the Miami-Dade District Attorney's Office? Who was my opponent? I learned that a seasoned and experienced prosecutor, Reid Ruben, would be fighting me in trial. I asked around. Scuttlebutt was that he had a reputation for being reasonable and fair. Good news. I called to start the talks.

It wasn't easy. Initially, Reid was not receptive at all to the mental health issues: he was viewing the promiscuity issue as the key to his case. He wasn't buying that Yvette was insane. This defined my first big chore: realizing that Reid clearly did not understand that Katherine's death was symptomatic of a major mental illness, I needed to educate him. Get him to see another viewpoint: one where he saw that it was not unusual for someone in Yvette's position to be sexually unrestrained for various reasons, including her state of mind and her capacity for judgment.

Over time, state attorney Reid Ruben became much more receptive to my arguments, especially as we shared the details of Dr. Amador's findings with him. Dr. Amador's reputation preceded him with Ruben, and the reality that Yvette was legally insane at the time of the crime became more viable to the prosecution once our expert's opinion was shared.

Maybe this isn't how things are done on television, but the reality is that prosecution and defense share evidence and reveal what they'll be introducing at trial long before a jury is picked. It's less dramatic this way, but it's better for our clients and it's better for the state, too. They don't want to try a case they're going to lose — and most prosecutors are seeking justice. Most state attorneys do want to be fair. Negotiations toward a plea were advancing.

This didn't mean that I wasn't preparing for trial. I was. As the lead attorney, I recognized that my one big weakness to overcome was Katherine. This would be the first time that I had defended someone accused of killing a child, or for that matter, anyone charged with that horrendous crime, much less a parent.

It was incumbent on me and my team to actually go out and learn as much as we could about the killing of a child. Why does it happen? When? What happened in past cases, here in Florida and elsewhere?

Research at the Library
In 1999 we didn't have the internet resources that are available to lawyers today. I soon found myself, with my pens and my yellow legal pads, over at the University of Miami medical library housed at Jackson Memorial Hospital. Hours, days, weeks passed as I worked my way through various journals and other research on the psychiatric and physiological issues concerning the killing by a parent of a child. Filicide, it's called.

What I discovered was an area that was wide open. Filicide is the killing of a child by a parent: there is maternal filicide and paternal filicide. I discovered that when a woman kills a child, it's rare, and very rare that she would do so in the circumstances that the state's theory was advancing. Maternal filicide is usually seen in circumstances involving significant mental health issues, delusional issues, reality issues, and issues that were related to the actual state of mind of the mother at the time that the killing occurs.

This research all flew in the face of the state's theory that Yvette Yallico was motivated to drown Katherine because of an unhappy marriage, wanting to get rid of the child so she could go on as a single woman, and have new relationships. This was a lot for me to digest and then master so that I could, in turn, explain what I had learned to the jury. This was just the starting point of all my research work.

Next, I spent significant time with my team really investigating the mental health aspects of schizophrenia and bipolar schizophrenic illness — the differences between the illnesses and the similarities. Why had Yvette been given so many different diagnoses? Why did she have overlapping, multiple diagnoses? What did all this mean?

The soft science aspect of psychology is much different, evidence-wise, from concrete science, like a blood test, for example. With blood work, you can go in and say, well, this person's blood is fraught with a disease and this is how we know it. With psychological evidence, proof boils down to an expert giving an opinion based on symptoms, history, and his or her own judgment. That human factor can always be argued to bring with it problems of misdiagnosis and misinterpretation.

Over time, it became clear: whether Yvette was schizophrenic or bipolar schizoaffective, she was clearly psychotic at the time. More important than the diagnosis, we needed to be able to explain the symptoms related to the diagnosis and how they played out in her behavior and in her killing of her child.

Discovering the Need for an Educational Expert

As files grew and time passed, one of the things we discovered was that the Florida school system had a very particular way of reaching the level of placement where Yvette ended up, in the "severely emotionally disturbed" category for the education component. We'd filed a public records request and found that the school had set up a procedure to identify troubled, mentally ill students, where they were marked, or labeled, and thereafter treated. It was a process that required multiple evaluations from multiple parties, all information that was very important to our defense.

Why? I would be arguing to Ruben (and the jury) here was evidence — piles of it — that the school system recognized early on that Yvette was a severely emotionally disturbed student. The school district expended significant funding to designate her as SED — this was substantiation of our position that she was legally insane.

However, no one on our team had the credentials to take all this paperwork and provide admissible evidence from it.

We needed another expert for that: an educational psychologist of sorts.

I retained a local psychologist who specialized in treating and testing students — and knew the intricacies of the process used to place Yvette in the school district's emotionally disturbed program. Could we have skipped this expense? No.

The importance of the experts cannot be underscored. In any capital case, you're going to have experts both in the first part of the case (the guilt or innocence part) and if necessary, the second part of the case (the penalty part). Most of the time, the experts don't overlap between these two phases of the case. The experts usually relate to specific areas of evidence, some of which applies to proving innocence and others that correspond to punishment.

In Yvette's defense, we would have some overlap. The experts in the first phase would end up being used directly or indirectly in the second phase; obviously, this was an integrated case where the integration of insanity would also play a role in both.

At trial, the jury would hear the insanity defense. If they decided not to acquit her or found her not guilty by reason of insanity, then in the second phase we would be making the argument that her mental illness is mitigation. Her illness was why the death penalty should not be part of the case at hand and why she should get life in prison as opposed to death.

Nixing the Accident Defense

I considered early on hiring an expert criminologist to deal with the issue of how long it took to fill the bathtub. That

became important early on because the investigators had
spent a significant time at the apartment of Yvette, filling and
refilling the bathtub, while they were trying to make a determination of the consistency of her story.

Yvette had said that she had put the baby in the bathtub.
She left the water on and went to cook. When she came back,
the child had slipped and was floating in the water, and that's
when she called her husband, so the filling and un-filling of
the bathtub had become important in terms of timing in
making a determination of what defense I was going to use.

Instead of immediately hiring an expert, I had my investigator go out to the apartment. He was allowed by the land-
lord to fill and un-fill the bathtub. We did our own recreation
and videotaped for possible exploration of the alternative
accident defense. If we went with this argument, we'd need to
hire more experts — something ultimately we decided not to
do because of the insanity issue.

It's one of the hard calls that lawyers have to make. At
first, Yvette had said that the drowning was an accident.
She'd given two statements to the police that the death was
accidental, and until the one-on-one confab she had with the
homicide sergeant, the police had intended to charge her with
negligent manslaughter.

An accident defense was there. We'd have to argue that
the confession was false, and that it was the result of pressure
from the homicide expert. It would be an evidence fight.

However, the bigger hurdle was the fact that Yvette left
the child in the bathtub. After the killing, Yvette did not
remove Katherine's body from the tub. When her husband
arrived at the scene, the child was floating in the bathtub.

This made absolutely no sense from an accident-defense perspective: a distraught mother finding her baby motionless in the water would have done something; just pulling the child out would have been a real life reaction — not leaving the baby there. No. We shouldn't argue the accident defense, even if there was one technically on the table: what we had was insanity. Why would a sane person, even a person who is trying to cover up a crime, not take the child out and pretend that they are trying to do some kind of intervention?

By leaving the child in the bathtub, it really fostered the support that this woman was not in her right mind; she was not planning or scheming to kill this child; and it was not intentional killing. In fact, leaving the baby there became symbolic to some extent of some of the things that Yvette babbled about later: telling her doctors that her child could come back if she prayed enough.

This was a legal insanity defense case, square on the money, and the team would have to move forward with this as our core argument. Some on the team considered Yvette's sanity a non-issue from the start, considering she was on the scene, showing no emotion, not crying, not being upset; when she was placed in the police vehicle downstairs she was interviewed and she basically was asking when she could wrap this up so she could go study for a test.

She just didn't make sense, didn't make sense at all. Which led us to the decision we had to make within a short period — were we going to put a waiver package together in terms of the death penalty?

The Waiver Package

What is a waiver package? A waiver package is a presentation through some form, usually written, with supporting documentation explaining to the state attorney's office why the case at hand is not a death penalty case (despite the decision they made already) and why they should take the death penalty off the table.

Death should no longer be an option, we would argue: they should withdraw their notice to seek the death penalty and proceed with this case as a non-death penalty case. If we succeeded, the state would waive capital punishment as an option in sentencing.

Getting that waiver is important for many reasons. One, you don't want a death-qualified jury hearing the case. Death-qualified juries are known to be more prone to convict. Second, obviously you don't want to put your client at risk of the death penalty. Finally, prosecutors sometimes use the death penalty as a bargaining chip in plea negotiations and you want to get rid of the chance that your client may feel forced to take a plea based on his or her terror of a possible death sentence.

The waiver package is something that has to be approached strategically because in Florida, discovery is very liberal. Florida criminal procedure requires the defense provide the prosecutor with any documents, experts, reports, statements, etc. that the defense plans on using in trial — either the penalty phase or guilt phase — just as the state is required to provide those documents to you.

Legally, the question isn't IF you have to turn things over, but WHEN you have to do it. Many times, you will not provide documents until much later in the case or you will hold those documents and file Motions for Protective Order to preclude having to turn over those documents until after the guilt phase.

Many times, you don't want to provide those documents because they are going to put your client at risk for some reason. The waiver package is jam-packed full of documentation, so there is a strategic component in deciding whether to provide a waiver package or not. You can't shut that barn door after the horse is gone.

In Yvette's case, it was not necessary within the first year and a half of the case to decide on the Waiver Package because of the mental illness component, and the communication I had already begun having with the prosecutor. Reid Ruben recognized that given Yvette's age and her severe mental health issues, he had a very weak leak to any aggravating factors to support a death sentence. My position was that Ruben had no aggravating factors: even taking a theoretical approach — that it was a cold, calculated, and premeditated murder, and heinous, atrocious, and cruel — the mental illness reality trumped that argument.

As our talks continued, I realized that the state did not have a hardcore dedication to move forward with the death penalty in this case. I used it to the advantage I could legally, delaying turning over documents as long as I could. I wanted to keep chatting, because Yvette's insanity would become real to Ruben given enough time. The waiver package might hurt the tenor and tone of our chats, taking things to a different level.

Prosecutors as Formidable Opponents or Partners in Finding Justice

In this kind of case, the prosecutors are usually the best of the best; they are the top dogs of their field. Usually they bring a different approach and different evaluation aspect. Here, as in many other death penalty cases, the prosecutor did his homework. Ruben spent a lot of time preparing. He spent a lot of time with the investigators, understanding and knowing every detail of this case. He spent a lot of time with the witnesses, including the husband of the client. Juan wasn't talking to Yvette now, no visits, and he was having very little communication with her by letters. Juan was keeping a hands-off approach.

The prosecutor knew this case inside and out, and while Juan might be his more important witness, for me, my most important witness became Dr. Xavier Amador. It was through Dr. Amador's expert analysis that I would be able to show that at the time of the homicide, Yvette Yallico was insane, consistent with Florida Law: that she had a mental defect that was active and because of that, she was unable to distinguish right from wrong.

We traveled to New York City so the state could depose Dr. Amador. In preparation for his deposition, we spent a significant amount of time discussing all the records, witness statements, police records, and all the possible areas of questioning the prosecution might choose. Ruben was prepared, as I knew he would be. A deposition that would normally take a couple of hours lasted an entire day. It was the turning point.

Ultimately, it was the deposition testimony given by Dr. Amador that day that facilitated the most important decision in this case: whether to go to trial or to plea the case. Reid Ruben and I began discussing what was the fairest possible outcome — where was justice here?

Plea Negotiations

The defense team didn't see the Yallico case as without worry if we took this to a trial. Team members were troubled by some of the implications in some supporting evidence. These include Yvette making multiple statements over a long period, even when she wasn't psychotic, that she was unhappy about having a child at such a young age, and that she was unhappy about being forced to marry her husband. The team also fretted over what a jury might think about Yvette being involved in extramarital relationships, some of which were outside the times when she was obviously psychotic. There were witnesses, schoolmates, who would tell the jury that Yvette talked about having a crush on a boy, and this was six months to a year before the murder. Would the jury think this suggested premeditation?

So we were troubled, and I of course was troubled by the idea of having to present an insanity defense on its face. Insanity is a difficult defense. To win, you must persuade the jury to allow someone who they believe is defective to escape punishment and, or more importantly, to be able to do what they did again. Essentially the jury has to be able to say that even though she is mentally ill, and she may do this again if she doesn't take her medication, we're not going to hold her legally culpable because she is not legally culpable, according to Florida Statute. That's a difficult thing for a jury to do.

Try the case, go for a deal? Going for a jury verdict is a difficult risk to present to a client who is barely competent at any given time. Yvette would have to understand and discuss the consequences of all the things that we are discussing now in this chapter.

The Plea Offer

In the midst of all this debate, we had to make the call. Dr. Amador's deposition led to the presentation by the prosecutor of a plea offer.

And, as part of that plea offer, came the acknowledgment that Juan, Yvette's husband and Katherine's father, agreed to this deal. While I'm not saying this was because he was partly responsible for the homicide, Juan clearly allowed Yvette to manipulate him — or he manipulated her. Who knows what the situation was in allowing her to be released from Jacksonville Memorial when she was psychotic. This was only six or seven months before Katherine died. Add to that the bad fact that Yvette was released against medical advice, and ultimately Juan's got to come full circle: his knowingly psychotic wife who he got out of the hospital killed his child.

Pointing the finger at Juan didn't negate that Yvette lied in two of her statements. She had lied about this being an accident, and I felt this would trouble a jury. Would they think that if she had enough wherewithal to think up an excuse, then she wasn't all *that* insane that day? It was a troubling fact — I could deal with it in trial, but it bothered me.

Ultimately, the prosecutor offered a 15-year plea sentence. After some negotiating back and forth, we agreed on a 15-year plea sentence followed by extensive probation and the condition that her work would not ever allow her to be unsupervised with children. The defense team agreed this was a reasonable result in this case. We felt it was a victory in the face of a true tragedy.

I had to sit down and get Yvette to understand things. This was a hard chore to perform, but Yvette came to comprehend and agree with me. I thought that the 15-year plea offer was reasonable in light of all the circumstances, and although I truly believe she was insane at the time, I wasn't so sure the jury would agree with that — so the 15-year plea offer was accepted.

Most cases never go to trial and end in plea deals. There is even a special hearing in which the judge goes through a set of questions, called the plea colloquy, before accepting the defendant's guilty plea. "Are you satisfied with your attorney?" "Do you understand that you are giving up a right to trial, a right to appeal?" "Is there a factual basis for your guilty plea?" "No one forced you to take this plea?"

Yvette's plea colloquy was one of the saddest I have ever seen. While Yvette was offered a very good plea, it was sad because at the plea she looked so young. Yvette was very nervous and was shaking as she raised her right hand. No one from her family was present. She literally took the plea alone.

It's now 2010 as I dictate these memories, and Yvette Yallico is set to be released shortly.

Chapter Two:
Childhood Abuse

SOMETIME AFTER MY representation of Yvette Yallico, I was appointed to represent another defendant accused of killing his child. However, this time it was the child's father who the state of Florida had charged with first degree murder. The state was asking for the sentence of death. My client was a young man, Victor Robinson. He was accused of killing his eight-month-old son by stomping him, shaking him, and kicking him as the baby lay on an apartment's carpet while Victor was in a jealous rage.

Once again, I came on board after the Florida Public Defender had initially begun representing the defendant, and as usual, I was stepping into a defense that had been phenomenally prepared. Their social worker, Marlene Schwartz, had done an especially exceptional job in working up the forensic background of the case. I still remember how thorough her files were. I also recall how those records proved to be crucial in my efforts to defend Mr. Robinson, because I was facing a prosecutor fiercely refusing to consider any waiver of the death penalty.

After putting together a defense team in a manner similar to the Yallico group, my goal was to establish that there were sufficient reasons for the prosecution to reconsider its stance on capital punishment. My role here, and truly in any death penalty case where guilt is not an issue is simple. I'm not trying to excuse what's happened; I'm trying to explain it.

The case of Victor Robinson, as I quickly learned from the work product provided by the Florida Public Defender and confirmed in our further defense efforts, was that substantial and severe mental disabilities were present here. Mr. Robinson suffered from mental challenges that legally and ethically should prevent his execution.

Getting a prosecutor to see this viewpoint, or getting a jury to agree with my perspective, would be very difficult. Any case where a baby has been killed is horrific, and emotions are high. As a father, I cringed as I worked the case, and my boys probably got a bit of extra care and attention during that time. I understood that the circumstances surrounding this death were shocking, and it would take some effort to get eyes to move away from that scene to a consideration of Victor Robinson's reality.

Unlike Yvette Yallico, the case of Victor Robinson provides a prime example of how childhood trauma directly affects an adult's reactions and his adult behavior. It is true that an individual's horrific childhood experiences can reach far into the future, sparking mental and emotional reactions and thereby controlling their sometimes tragic consequences.

Knowing the complete history of Victor Robinson, the death
of that tiny baby, eight-month-old Kelton Robinson, seemed
almost inevitable — like a movie where you've already figured
out the ending. Here's the story.

Victor and Ciji Fall In Love

Around the time that I was taking on the Yallico representation, back in 1999, Victor Robinson met Ciji Wright and they
began to date. Ciji thought Victor was nice, so different from
her previous boyfriends.

Indeed, Victor was much more different than Ciji could
have known at the time. During our defense investigation of
Victor's background, interviewing scores of witnesses and
culling through boxes and boxes and cabinets full of school
records, medical records, and the like, we learned of the tragic
beginnings for this boy: Victor had been born to a drug-
addicted prostitute, and from the time he was very little until
he was around the age of ten years old, he watched his
mother turn tricks and do drugs on a daily basis.

Around the time that Victor turned nine, his mother did
the unthinkable: she changed her life and her son's as well.
Victor's mother was born-again, and she broke her addictions
to drugs and alcohol. Life was different in many ways, good
ways, now that Mrs. Robinson was attending church and
abstaining from intoxicants; still, the lives of mother and son
were psychologically intertwined.

Then, like an intervening miracle, Victor was discovered
to have exceptional musical talent in high school. By the time
he turned 18 years old, he had a mentor, charter school

advances, and a promising future. Victor Robinson, the son of a backstreet prostitute, was awarded a scholarship to a local community college to pursue his musical talents. Victor had a future. And it was in this bright light that Victor met and fell in love with Ciji.

The romance blossomed. Victor and Ciji went out to the movies a lot, talked on the phone for hours, and became very close. They were in love, as only the very young can be. In 2001, Ciji became pregnant with Victor's first child. The couple was happy about the pregnancy and looked forward to building a family. However, in May 2001, Ciji had a miscarriage; their child was stillborn.

Victor was particularly devastated by the loss. The couple grieved, but soon decided to try again. They had made plans for the future together, and they wouldn't give up now. Ciji and Victor wanted a family.

In August 2001, Victor left to go to Tallahassee to attend school. It was part of their plan. However, in just a few weeks, Victor had given up school and returned home because of another crisis: Victor's mother, who had been sick for some time, had taken a turn for the worse.

Victor's mother had recovered from her addiction to drugs and alcohol, but not before she had contracted AIDS. She died from AIDS on October 10, 2001. Victor lost his mother less than six months after he had lost his child.

After Mrs. Robinson's funeral, Ciji started to notice that Victor was behaving strangely. As time passed, she noticed significant changes in Victor — scary ones, and ones which ultimately resulted in the two of them breaking up.

Unbeknownst to Ciji when the couple split, she was pregnant with their second child. When Ciji told Victor she was pregnant, he retorted that he doubted whether or not the child was his anyway. Ciji moved back home with her parents and prepared to have the baby.

Ciji carried the baby to term without Victor; he wasn't by her side now like he'd been when she was pregnant the first time. They had very little contact throughout her pregnancy, and Victor wasn't there when Kelton Robinson was born on June 10, 2002. Ciji listed Victor as the baby's father on the birth certificate, and after she brought the baby home, she invited Victor to be a part of the child's life. Maybe they wouldn't be a couple, but maybe they would still be co-parents.

Kelton is Born

It was through Kelton's arrival that Ciji and Victor became reacquainted. During our interviews, Ciji still remembered watching Victor's face when she introduced him to his son, and how Victor looked upon Kelton in "amazement," talking with Ciji about how he wanted to be part of their child's life. Victor was happy that day as only new, young fathers can understand.

But Victor wasn't like other young fathers. Ciji's mother was fearful of Victor Robinson; she thought he was danger-ous. Ciji's mother did not want Victor spending time either with her daughter or grandson, and she told him so. She refused to let Victor in her home, and she forbid her daughter from having anything to do with Victor. Nevertheless, Ciji would sneak Victor into the house so he could visit with Kelton. And so they could be together: the love affair between Ciji and Victor had reignited.

That this situation blew up wasn't a surprise to anyone. Discovered, the couple refused to part. Now they were a family. Taking their son, Ciji and Victor moved into a hotel together. Almost immediately, the atmosphere changed.

Ciji began to be aware of the paranoia and jealously displayed by Victor; she began to realize why her mother was so concerned. At the hotel, Victor would get jealous of any man he saw in the area — in the parking area, on the sidewalk — and he was constantly rushing Ciji behind closed doors, or trying to keep her inside their room.

Even more frightening, Ciji watched as Victor would talk to Kelton, too small to walk or talk, conversing with the baby as though the child understood all that Victor was saying. Ciji became very afraid, and after living in the hotel room for only a short time, Ciji and Victor broke up a second time. Ciji took Kelton and went back home to her mother.

This separation lasted for a few months. The split, in September 2002, was over by Christmas. In December, Ciji's mother kicked her out of the house — tough love — for a short time, because Victor had begun to show up at the house to spend time with Ciji and Kelton. The couple, perhaps in the spirit of the holiday season, had mended fences again: in February 2003, Ciji, Victor, and Kelton moved into an apartment together.

The Family Moves Into an Apartment Together

Over the holidays, Ciji noticed that Victor had taken up a
new hobby: he was smoking marijuana daily. She soon
became aware that Victor was not only smoking marijuana,
but he was buying "dirty" marijuana, where cocaine is mixed
with the herb and smoked. Ciji thought that Victor's drug use
was affecting his behavior and making it worse than it was
before.

More and more, Victor was paranoid about losing Ciji.
He was terrified she would leave him. Victor was exhibiting
jealous and controlling behavior more and more frequently.
Things were escalating, too. Now, Victor would not allow Ciji
to talk to family members or friends. Whenever Ciji walked to
the store for a few things, she would feel his eyes on her;
Victor watched her every move.

Inside the apartment, Victor was angrier than he'd ever
been. He became abusive toward her and argued with Ciji
constantly, sometimes over nonsensical things. Then, there
was the first incident involving the baby. As the couple was
fighting, Kelton was hurt. It would happen one month before
the death.

The fight began while Victor was acting in the erratic
behavior consistent with him smoking "dirty" marijuana, and
as their anger fueled itself, Victor began to hit Ciji. The baby
was crying; Victor placed a sock into the child's mouth to
keep him quiet. Somehow, in all of this, Victor hit the baby
— but he and Ciji both testified this was also the only time he
had ever struck the child, and the hit was intended for Ciji; he
wasn't aiming for the infant.

The police were called to the apartment, as well as Children and Family Services. No charges were filed after all the interviews were held at the scene. The baby was not removed from the home.

Instead, Victor was referred to and agreed to complete parenting classes and anger management sessions. He attended them. Victor also showed remorse for his actions. He felt bad about hitting the baby and Ciji.

The Day the Baby Died

Nevertheless, during this period of time, Victor's paranoia grew. His jealousy and fear of losing Ciji became bizarre. Now, Victor began to direct his comments of jealousy toward Kelton. Ciji tried to explain that Kelton was Victor's son, but Victor felt shunned by the infant, telling her that Kelton did not act like "I'm his father." Victor complained that Kelton wasn't showing him any attention; the baby cared only about Ciji. Kelton, an eight-month-old, suddenly took on significant power within the household, in Victor's perceptions.

On March 3, 2002, the day of the fatal incident, Victor started another fight with Ciji. The argument began, according to neighborhood witnesses, because Victor saw Ciji leaving the apartment of a male neighbor who Victor suspected that she was having an affair with at the time. Victor was furious.

Accusing her of being unfaithful, again, Victor began to refer to Kelton, too. He told Ciji that she had to "choose" between him and Kelton. Victor was at the boiling point. Ciji would later describe how Victor was at a level of rage she had never seen before, that his eyes were "different." The argument continued. The more they argued, the more enraged he became.

As Victor exploded, he began assaulting Ciji. He kept yelling at her, "You told me you wouldn't put no other man before me, how could you do that to me, you told me to the day we die." They were both screaming.

Kelton, in his crib, started to cry. Ciji picked him up after the initial assault, only to have Victor grab Kelton away from Ciji and toss him on the bed. As they continued to argue, Ciji grabbed Kelton off of the bed. She tried to console the child.

As the baby boy continued to cry, an enraged and crazed Victor took the child from Ciji and began to shake Kelton, telling him to stop crying, just as he would an adult. Again, Ciji took the child away from Victor. Now, she took the baby and walked toward the bathroom to give the child a bath, attempting to de-escalate the argument.

Turning from him like this infuriated Victor even more. He grabbed the child while striking Ciji. He continued to rant, make the same statements repetitively, while assaulting the baby by dropping him on the floor, stomping him and hitting him. After the assault, as soon as possible, Ciji retrieved a neighbor who provided help by performing CPR on the baby. Kelton had stopped breathing and was resuscitated by the neighbor.

Someone called the police. Kelton was taken to the hospital, where he was taken off life support several days later. At the scene, police interviewed Victor. He told officers that he had lost his temper and had struck his child on the back with an open hand and admitted that he had a heavy hand.

Victor was arrested and charged with one count of first degree murder, one count of aggravated child abuse, and one count of simple battery. He was subsequently indicted for first degree murder and multiple counts of aggravated child abuse. Being indigent, the Florida Public Defender was promptly appointed to represent him.

Forensic Investigation Into Social History

Taking over for the Public Defender's Office meant that lots of work had been done to provide the facts that would explain why this death had occurred — but it was far from a done deal. Our defense team would have to spend hours, days, and weeks combing through records, meeting with people, making phone calls, and building relationships of trust with people who we knew would only tell embarrassing, perhaps socially taboo facts, if they believed we were worthy of that confidence. Learning Victor Robinson's sad story from the day he was born to the day he was arrested was a huge undertaking — if we wanted the unvarnished truth of it. And we did; without it, I couldn't mount a proper defense to keep him from execution.

Fitting together the puzzle pieces provided by investigators, social workers, paralegals, and attorneys, we discovered a compelling and heart-wrenching life. From birth, Victor had been burdened with a life filled with great disadvantage.

Born to a Drug Addicted Prostitute in 1981

He was born to Barbara Robinson — a heavy drug and alcohol user — on October 29, 1981, at Jackson Memorial Hospital. Victor's birth weight was five pounds; subsequent to his birth, Victor was hospitalized because he had a hernia. Records indicated that, during this period of time, his mother was considering placement (giving Victor up for adoption) because she had nowhere to live and was a cocaine user as well as a heavy drinker.

There in the hospital, Barbara decided to keep and raise Victor, but she still continued to use drugs until Victor was eight or nine years old. During this time, Victor not only witnessed her drug use, but on countless occasions he was brought to drug-infested apartment houses. Moreover, he witnessed his mother being solicited for prostitution daily; Victor was left nearby while she committed these acts, which supported her son, herself, and a serious drug habit.

Documented Abuse and Neglect

On one occasion, Victor was left at a bus bench all day while his mother spent hours in a car with various men. On another occasion, he was left with strangers while his mother visited a bar across the street.

Sometimes, he would stand by as his mother became embroiled in fights on the streets: violence over crack or johns or money. No one will ever know all the memories Victor carries with him, but psychologists will know the importance of one fact in particular: even as Victor entered his adolescent years, he would lose control of his bowels regularly.

As a young boy, Victor recalled his mother having "meetings" with men where she would lock herself in a room with them. Barbara was gay. She would describe men to be necessary as providers, to give one a roof over one's head — but she would never love them. Another childhood issue: how did this translate to her boy and how was he to assimilate this information?

In this atmosphere of lack, Victor experienced the loss of numerous family members (including his grandfather, grandmother, and uncle), some of whom died violent deaths. He had a large family, which included four sisters. His two older sisters, Tanisha and Bernice, were raised by their maternal grandmother, Bernice Fuller. They were taken from the hospital after birth. In fact, Barbara had told several people that she had kept Victor because she was intent on proving that she was getting better and could raise a child after she had lost custody of her first two children to her own mother. Victor lived alone with Barbara in a HUD apartment for some time.

Barbara did have two babies after having Victor. His two younger sisters, Tiffany and Rashida, were raised in part by relatives, in part by foster care, and occasionally by Barbara herself. When Victor's mother became clean and sober, after her release from rehabilitation, the younger sisters, Victor, and Barbara were reunited as a family. Victor was eight years old at the time the family moved in under one roof.

This transition was especially difficult for Victor. He had always had an extremely close relationship with his mother, being very protective of her during their time alone. Used to having all of his mother's attention, Victor became jealous of his sisters after the family reintegrated.

Series of Mental Illness Hospitalizations Beginning at Age 8

Unfortunately, the damage done to Victor — including experiencing the death of close family members, quickly became evident. Beginning at age eight, and periodically throughout his teen years, Victor was hospitalized at mental health facilities on numerous occasions.

During these hospitalizations, Victor told the doctors that his mother beat him using sticks and 2 by 4s. Victor had the scars to prove it. He ran away from home to avoid the beatings.

The mental health professionals would diagnose Victor with any number of things over the years, including: conduct disorder; aggressive, intermittent explosive disorder; depression recurrent with mood incongruent psychotic features; conduct disorder, solitary aggressive type; and organic personality disorder, explosive type.

Victor was given lots of drugs. As a child, he was prescribed Lithium Carbonate and Thorazine. A few years later, Victor was diagnosed with encopresis (he passed stools into his pants). Victor was enrolled in classes for the emotionally handicapped.

Early childhood test results on the WISC III (an intelligence test for children) concluded that he had a full scale IQ

of 73 (borderline). He was only 4 points away from the low-
est IQ level possible, "intellectually deficient."

Between February 9 and 12, 1993, Victor was placed on
suicide watch after indicating that he wanted to die. In addition, records noted he exhibited a thought disorder that led to
loose or fragmented thoughts, racing thoughts, poor judgment, poor reality testing, and magical thinking.

He also had moderate levels of auditory and visual hallucinations, poor self-concept, anxiety/panic reactions, and
mania. He was 11 years old.

Serious Drugs, Suicide Watches

More drugs. He was prescribed Haldol, Cogentin, Trilafon
and Trofranil. A few months later, in April of 1993, he was
hospitalized at Deering Hospital for one month and a half. At
Deering, Victor was diagnosed with Schizo-Affective Disorder Bi-Polar Type. He was described as having fragmented
thoughts, auditory hallucinations, and poor reality testing, as
well as being anxious and depressed. Victor was considered a
danger to himself, due to his poor impulse control. He spoke
of an imaginary man coming to his house during the night
and killing him.

Psychological records revealed that Victor rationalized
his mother's physical abuse by stating, "I don't mind it, it
means that she loves me." Not surprisingly, this boy struggled
with feelings of anger and trust, and had severe abandonment
issues. He was again placed on suicide watch. The hospital
documents stated that Victor's inability to handle life's stress-
ors was a significant problem.

Upon release from Deering, Victor was placed on Tofranil, Trilafon, and Cogentin. Throughout his schooling, Victor was involved in programs for the emotionally handicapped. He continued to be medicated. Toward the end of high school, Victor's behavior radically changed: music entered his life, and he graduated in 2000 with his high school diploma. After graduation, he held a number of jobs. Records revealed that Victor might have had a future in music.

August 2001, Victor at the Crossroads

In August 2001, he moved to Tallahassee and signed a lease on an apartment. Within a matter of weeks, Victor was faced with a life-changing decision to make: stay or go? His mother had become extremely ill. He abandoned his future, choosing to return to Miami to be with her. Then again, psychologically, maybe Victor had no choice.

Upon his return to Miami, Victor spent every waking moment caring for his mother — even sleeping with her — until her death on October 10, 2001. By all accounts, her death crushed him. He subsequently cared for his sick aunt for the next year until she passed away. Victor's compassion and tender care for both his mother and his aunt was significant to everyone who witnessed it. Victor was a "good boy."

The Plea Deal

After presenting the prosecution with all the details of Victor Robinson's life — beginning with his birth to where we were that day, at a negotiation table — we were able to come to an agreement. No trial. No death penalty.

What were the keys to changing the state attorney's mind about seeking capital punishment? Here it was the voluminous documentation of his upbringing, his social history, and his huge record of acknowledged mental illness. The combination of these factors supported Ciji's acknowledgment of the defendant's bizarre paranoia and rage about losing Ciji on the day that the baby died.

Legally, this became a case where "heinous, atrocious, or cruel" was factually inapplicable to this damaged defendant. I negotiated a plea with the state attorney. Today, Victor Robinson is serving 40 years imprisonment for the death of his son.

Chapter Three:
Mentally Challenged

THERE'S SOMETHING ALMOST magical in the way moonlight spreads itself over the ocean waves when you're walking at night along the sandy beaches here in South Florida. The sounds of the waves, the quiet breezes, the feel of the sand beneath your feet: romantic walks along the oceanfront here in Miami are something shared by tourists and natives alike. Memories are made here; perhaps you have a few. I hope this war story of mine doesn't ruin them for you.

Back in April 2002, a young high school couple had made moonlight walks along the beach a part of their routine: Ana Maria and Nelson would pick someplace inexpensive to have dinner and then they would drive to Miami Beach for the rest of their date night. The two teens, young and besotted, would stroll the beach together. Typical young lovers:

they never worried about being accosted or bothered — this was their magical time, where plans were made for the future.

Perhaps it was fate, maybe just being in the wrong place at the wrong time. Whatever your belief system, on that spring night in 2002, Ana Maria and Nelson weren't alone on that beach; they were being watched. There on the sand, walking back to their car hand-in-hand, the teenagers were confronted by three Latino males. It was dark, it was a remote area, and there wasn't anyone else around.

One of the men had a gun.

Joel Lebron stood there, pointing a pistol at the couple and demanding they go with him to a nearby pickup truck. The truck was parked on the street corner, a hundred feet from the beach. My client, Cesar Mena, was the driver of that truck. He sat in the cab, watching Ana Maria and Nelson being forced into the vehicle.

After being coerced into the truck, Cesar behind the wheel, Ana and Nelson were taken to a nearby gas station, where Ana was made to use her ATM card and fill up the truck with gas. Next stop: a local bank, where Cesar withdrew money from Ana's account after obtaining the ATM pin number from her. Now the four boys — Tico, Victor, Joel, and Cesar — had money and a full tank of gas.

What happened next was an event so horrifying and excruciating that it's hard to retell it now, much less consider what these young people must have felt at the time. Being a criminal defense attorney should never harden your heart to horror; when that happens, it's time to stop practicing criminal law.

The cruel truth is that on that night, back in April 2002, pretty little naïve Ana was repeatedly gang raped in that truck by three of these four men while they cruised around town. Nelson was forced to sit on the floor of the truck and watch his lovely Ana being repeatedly raped orally and anally. Cesar did not try to stop this; however, he did refuse to participate, even though he was offered numerous times to do so. He just drove and drove and drove.

Imagine the evil in the air that night. In that truck.

Time passed. They had no real destination. After what seemed to be an endless period of driving around Miami, the foursome drove north on I-95. At some point while Cesar was driving, he was ordered to pull over to the side of the road. It was dark; there wasn't much traffic on the highway.

After the pickup had slowed to a stop, Nelson was removed from the truck by the two of the men and taken to the side of the road. Standing there beside the asphalt of I-95, listening to Ana crying inside the truck, Nelson was stabbed repeatedly by Victor and Joel. Falling to the ground, Nelson began bleeding profusely as the men crawled back into the truck, leaving the teenager on the side of the road to die.

Cesar was told to keep driving. They continued north on I-95 for just a bit before Joel told Cesar to once again stop the truck. Now, they pulled over about two miles north from where Nelson had been left for dead.

Joel Lebron and his two cohorts took Ana out of the truck, walking her slowly to the side of the highway and placing her on her knees, in a praying position. As Cesar watched, while Ana was begging for her life, Joel placed the cold nozzle of his firearm against her head and pulled the trigger. The men then piled back into the truck and drove toward Orlando. Once they got there, they divided the spoils of the ATM robbery and split up, each going their separate way.

These four individuals started making their bad choices the day before, when Cesar and his new friends had piled into the pickup truck to drive from their hometown of Orlando to Miami so they could buy marijuana. They got ripped off; the deal went bad to the tune of $600, and they were angry about it. Insulted. Disrespected.

The next day, the four men were back on the road, driving south from Orlando to Miami, blood boiling at the drug dealers who had shafted them. The deal would be made good; they would confront the dealers and get what was owed. Make things right.

Problem was, those drug dealers were nowhere to be found. The four drove around Miami for the better part of the day, draining their gas tank, and never could find the guys. Frustrated, egos blown and blood rising, they pulled their pickup truck into that parking lot on Miami Beach the night as Ana Maria and Nelson were coming back to their car.

It is probably no surprise to anyone that the four men were high. They had been smoking pot and drinking beer all day. What little inhibitions they may have had were definitely compromised by intoxicants that night when they decided on a whim to abduct the young couple with the intent to rob and obtain property from them.

Perhaps their inebriation had one benefit: they hadn't stabbed Nelson well enough to kill him. While the truck was on the road back to Orlando, Nelson stumbled to the side of

I-95 and flagged down a passing motorist. One call to 911, and Miami police along with a multi-jurisdictional police force became involved within a very short period of time.

The police were able to track the vehicle back to Orlando. Soon, all four individuals were arrested and behind bars, including my client, Cesar Mena.

Cesar was the first one to give a statement. With great remorse, he relived the moments that led up to the ending of Ana Maria's life. He sobbed throughout most of his statement, repeatedly telling the police that he felt pressured to do what he did, he didn't have a choice, and he didn't want anyone to get hurt. In his confession, Cesar was adamant that he did not participate in the rapes of Ana Maria, and he was repentant for what had happened to this young woman and her boyfriend. His actions supported his remorsefulness: Cesar worked with law enforcement, directing the police to the location where Ana had been dumped. Law enforcement found the body of Ana Maria where Cesar said they would: there, beside I-95, she lay with her hands folded in a praying position, a bullet lodged in her brain.

Within hours after the police located Ana's fragile body on the side of I-95, Cesar and his three pals had been arrested and charged with first degree murder. No one doubted that the state of Florida would seek the death penalty.

Now came the time in the judicial process where the lawyers were chosen. There was a short multi-jurisdictional dispute between Broward County and Miami-Dade County on who would prosecute the case, but it was ultimately decided that Abe Laeser, a seasoned and well-known trial lawyer for the Dade State Attorney's office, would take lead in both the investigation and ultimately in the prosecution of all four defendants.

On the defense side, Eric Cohen, a lawyer that I had worked with on numerous cases, was brought in as lead counsel in defending Cesar Mena. Shortly thereafter, I was appointed as the penalty phase lawyer. Cohen defends against guilt; Lenamon fights for mercy.

The formal death notices were summarily filed against all four defendants. Paperwork necessary for pursuing capital punishment; the notice is public record of the prosecution's intent.

With the notices, the state of Florida hit a roadblock: one of the four defendants was really a juvenile, and while it was understood he had participated in the killing, he was not death-qualified because of his age. In Florida, as in the rest of the United States, the punishment of death can only be sought against someone who is over 18 years old. Tico was sixteen years old at the time.

Anyone wanting an eye for an eye in this case had to look at the remaining three for their vengeance; as a minor, the death notice for Tico was void.

I knew that the state would be fighting all that more fiercely to kill Cesar Mena, now that Tico was out of the picture, and it was my sworn duty to prevent that from happening. This is the goal of the defense in the penalty phase. I began to assemble a team of investigators and mental health experts to assist me in preparing for trial. With Nelson's survival, and Cesar's own statements, it was more or less insured that guilt would be found, and trying a penalty phase would happen.

I met with my client. I started talking to potential witnesses, gathering facts. It wasn't long before I realized that
that Cesar was slow and there may be a legal issue of mental
retardation, the phrase used by the United States Supreme
Court in their determination that it is cruel and unusual punishment to execute the mentally challenged.

I hired an initial expert, Dr. Haber, to evaluate Cesar
Mena. Dr. Haber would turn out to be my throw-away witness — I ended up using her and listing her in discovery
responses to the state, even though her conclusions were
different from my main testifying expert. Mercy for Cesar
Mena depended upon a solid determination that he was
indeed legally mentally retarded, and we had to have a
renowned national expert on this issue. In time, I found one
in North Carolina, and we hired a very well-known doctor
and psychologist named Antonio Puentes to join the team.

My first major fight to urge the mitigating factor of
mental retardation would not wait until trial, however. A
Florida rule of criminal procedure offered an opportunity to
file a motion with the judge long before trial requesting an
order precluding the application of the death penalty for
Cesar Mena based on mental retardation. Strategically, I could
file a written request for this ruling long before any trial
began. This was the thing to do, and our team began working
hard to get ready to file that request and win that hearing.

What became problematic early on was applying the
rule's requirements to the unique circumstances surrounding
Cesar Mena. The Florida rule required that we prove that
Cesar had had some kind of diagnostic test regarding onset
mental retardation with a conclusion that prior to age 18 his

IQ was below 70, and that there were facts demonstrating a depth of behavior (or lack thereof) that was consistent with someone who is mentally retarded. It was a three-pronged test that usually posed no problem for our investigative team.

In short, the law requires evidence of mental retardation that was documented prior to age 18. Not a problem with the Florida school system, but Cesar Mena was born and raised in Honduras. We would have to rely on school records from Honduras, and we were finding that their records were not only substandard, but they were also incomplete.

Our investigators worked with Honduran officials and discovered that Cesar's education stopped at the 6th grade and that he had left Honduras at the age of 16; Cesar never had any other education. From 1st grade to 6th grade, Cesar attended a rural county school in La Ceiba, Honduras, and there was no record made that would have been consistent with testing required to establish the mental retardation legal issue. They didn't exist. As a result, our reliance on our testifying expert grew and grew the more we learned of the scant amount of Honduran documentation.

Dr. Puentes worked hard for Cesar Mena, and through testing he was able to confirm that Cesar had an IQ of 69. Next, of course, we ran into more problems. We had to prove adapted behavior problems, but Cesar's work and his ability to come across the border from Honduras when he was 16 years old could be used by the state attorney to hammer on the adapted behavior requirement, arguing to the judge that this prong of the three pronged test was not met.

What are adapted behaviors and how do you prove them? Adapted behaviors essentially are evidence that demonstrates a person can live independently of someone else. For example, if someone like Cesar can pay his rent, or if someone like Cesar could take a bus somewhere to shop, then this is evidence of adapted behavior. This evidence goes against a finding of legal mental retardation as a bar to capital punishment.

We needed detailed facts about Cesar's life, from childhood to arrest. It would be difficult: we were dealing with language barriers and international borders. Travel expense would be a factor; investigation would be complex and frustrating. Our defense evidence was in Honduras — that was the bottom line.

The big fact we knew at the get-go was that Cesar Mena had successfully crossed the border, coming to the United States from Honduras. That seems like an independent, capable task. However, from Florida we were able to provide evidence that Cesar was actually brought across the border by someone who was paid by his family. A coyote escorted Cesar Mena from Honduras to Florida. That's a different situation. Cesar didn't lead the way across the border; he followed.

We had to travel to Honduras. With our investigator, Maria Ortega, I flew on a regular plane and then on a small puddle jumper across the mountains of La Ceiba. Along the way, the tiny plane almost ran out of gas in mid-flight, which was an experience neither Maria nor I will ever forget.

After landing in La Ceiba, we met with numerous Mena family members, ready to help. Together, we collected records, and gathered a childhood history by combining numerous interviews with family members and friends. We learned that Cesar was abandoned by his mother when he was a small tot, and that other family members took over caring for him. We were also able to track down some health records that showed that Cesar had been hospitalized when he was very young. Sadly, during this Honduran hospitalization, Cesar apparently had an issue of deprivation of oxygen, which may have affected his brain to some extent, causing brain damage. More documentation for our expert's consideration, he would have to opine if these medical records did reveal an explanation for Cesar's mental limitations.

The Honduras trip was long, hard, and frustrating. There were rabbit trails, heat and humidity, and bad food with not enough Pepto Bismol. Ultimately, we were able to bring back to Florida nine family members willing to testify on behalf of Cesar. Back at the office, team members had to find hotels and transportation for our guests — and help them deal with cosmopolitan Miami, which proved at times to be overwhelming for them.

After Honduras, the investigative part of the defense job was winding down, and the need to build a strategy for presenting our defense began. Our hearing before the trial judge requesting that the death penalty be taken off the table was denied. The judge wanted a jury to decide Cesar's fate. It wasn't a surprise to us; our team had been building a trial mindset all along. We were going to trial.

Our theory was an integrated trial, meshing the guilt phase and the penalty phase, where the defense is not that you are denying that a person actually was involved in the crime; instead, you are arguing that the defendant was somehow lesser involved than what the prosecution is alleging.

This integration strategy became important because with the facts we knew would be coming into evidence, our defense had to be that our client, Cesar Mena, while present at the crime, was not a participant in the crime itself. This position was supported by a lot of evidence.

Importantly, our team had compiled a significant amount of witness testimony, as well as documentation showing that Cesar was a follower. He was easily led, he preferred this and looked for it. Additionally, we documented his low intelligence level, his childhood history where he lived without parents from a very young age, and also his limited education. Combine these factors together, and a picture came into focus of an individual more susceptible to peer pressure and less able to make concrete decisions that were important to be made. Our defense case was solidifying, becoming stronger by the day.

Then, from the outset, we had to deal with rising, significant pretrial publicity. The right of the media to cover criminal trials is valid and inviolate; however, with modern technology and the current trend on the part of some segments of the media to tantalize readers and viewers with sensationalism, the right of a defendant to get a fair trial can be jeopardized.

Before Cesar Mena's trial, his co-defendant Victor had been tried, found guilty, and received a death recommendation and death sentence. Cesar's trial would be next. Having to be the second defendant to go to trial was disconcerting, and we litigated the pretrial issue publicity to the extent that we could — asking the judge for help — and we also spent a lot of time focusing on the publicity issue during jury selection.

Would we be able to get jurors who were not prejudiced by what they had already learned about the case through media coverage? In any death penalty case, jury selection is an essential part of any possibility of obtaining a life-sentence recommendation. Whether the government has the right to execute humans as a sentence for a crime is a controversial issue built on moral, religious, and political considerations. Publicity adds another layer of complexity to a complex issue.

In Florida, it takes seven jurors to vote for death. We are not a state that requires a unanimous verdict. From a defense perspective, our goal in jury selection was to find six jurors who are going to vote for life under the circumstances of our case, and then empower them to do that very thing. We would have to give them, through evidence at trial, factual information that would support a conclusion that life would be a just verdict over a death sentence. And we would have to do this, fighting against perceptions already created in the media, which at the minimum might be sensationalized, and at the maximum, were downright false.

It took us two weeks to pick our jury. Not an unusual amount of time, considering the caliber of the case and the extensive pretrial publicity. During the jury selection, it was interesting that some of the jurors had individuals in their family who were suffering from either low intelligence issues, ADHD issues, or mental retardation issues. Was this more prevalent in our American culture than I realized?

One of our jurors had a brother who was mentally retarded. Even now, I think that this one person's experience became an important part in Cesar escaping a death sentence. That compassion and firsthand knowledge of how life can be for someone who is mentally challenged cannot be underestimated.

Of course, the key to our defense was the opinion of Dr. Puentes, our bilingual testifying expert from North Carolina. Dr. Puentes determined that Cesar Mena was mentally retarded and in his testimony, clearly and respectfully took the jury through the three prongs required in the process of legally evaluating mental retardation.

He pointed out the fact that Cesar Mena was a follower, easily influenced by his friends. Dr. Puentes explained how and why Cesar had an inability to make the concrete decisions most of us make daily and just take for granted that we have the capability to do so.

Dr. Puentes also explained how Cesar was unable to resist the peer pressures that were present during the night of the event, based upon this combination of factors. Because of Cesar's upbringing and his limited IQ abilities, Cesar was simply unable to resist the leadership qualities of some of the other members of the group that night, where not only did they rape Ana Maria, but they also stabbed Nelson and shot Ana. It was a major achievement for Cesar to decline their repeated attempts to get him to join them in their sexual batteries.

It was a tough trial. The state's testifying expert shocked everyone by contradicting himself and changing his test results. The media coverage was heavy and unrelenting.

Finally, the defense rested the penalty phase late one Thursday evening, and the jury took over to deliberate.

Prayers were answered when they came back and recommended a life sentence without the possibility of parole for Cesar Mena. Cesar would live the rest of his life, and die, in a Florida state prison — but he would not be executed.

After they rendered their life recommendation, many of the jurors broke down in tears and proceeded to hug both Ana's mother in the hallway as well as Cesar's family members, who were standing nearby. It was a moment where mercy was personified that I will never forget, and one reason that I do this job.

Chapter Four:
Childhood Neglect

MIAMI HAS BEEN the setting for more than one popular television series based on crime — and there will probably be more. After all, Miami-Dade is a cosmopolitan place in
a beautiful setting. Juxtaposing the horrors of homicide
against the blue skies and green palms of Miami Beach provides good drama. Still, no matter how graphic these shows
become with their forensic gore and lifelike crime scenes,
they pale in comparison to the real homicides that happen
here.

Like the murder of young Jack Wray.

On May 4, 2001, the body of Jack Wray was discovered
behind the wheel of his burned Mitsubishi Eclipse on the side
of SW 87 Avenue, at approximately SW 240th Street if you
know the area. His body was burnt beyond recognition. The
heat of that fire had to be extremely intense to accomplish
turning a human body to this level of char. Experts would be

needed not only to figure how, but when, he died. Just like the crime shows, the police needed forensic expertise; the body was turned over to the Medical Examiner, Dr. Emma Lew.

Dr. Lew performed an autopsy on the remains of Jack Wray. She determined that the decedent had died from blunt trauma to the head and that mercifully, his death occurred before the fire. It was not clear what caused the head trauma; the police were unable to identify a murder weapon.

It could be a tedious investigation. The detectives changed their focus from the crime scene to the friends of the decedent. Someone would know something about why Jack Wray was dead. It might take a while to put things together.

Two days later, there was a break in the case. On May 7, 2001, police officers responded to a domestic call at the apartment of Feilberto Flores and Jessica Zelaya. During standard police questioning, the couple revealed that they had information about the death of Jack Wray.

Flores told the cops that along with his girlfriend Jessica and him, several other people lived in the apartment, including 17-year-old Jacob Zayas, 23-year-old Anthony Lopez, Jessica's sister Christina, and the children of both Jessica and Christina. A packed house, where making rent was easier the more people shared the load.

Jacob Zayas was there because Flores acted as Zayas' guardian; Flores received money every month from Zayas' mother to cover that expense. As for why Anthony Lopez was living there, it was a similar story of Flores finding help in covering the bills.

Flores met Lopez while he was working at Albertson's, a local grocery store, where Flores worked as a night stockman and Lopez cleaned the floors. They became friends, and around three months before the body of Jack Wray was discovered, Lopez had moved into the Flores apartment. It was good deal for everyone to share expenses.

Anthony Lopez met Jacob Zayas after they began sharing an apartment. It was Zayas who introduced Lopez to his teenaged friend Jack Wray. How that introduction resulted in the death of Jack Wray was murky at first; Flores initially lied to police until confronted with his girlfriend's version of events. Flores was visibly scared.

Flores told police that Jacob Zayas and Jack Wray had known each for over a year, and that they argued constantly, usually about God. Wray had found God; Zayas carried a grudge against God. And no, the two could not avoid quarreling just by avoiding religion; Flores said they would get into it over the stupidest things. Jacob and Jack just liked to bicker.

On the day of Wray's death, Flores had a doctor's appointment that kept him away from the apartment until around 7:30 p.m., where he arrived to find Jacob Zayas, Anthony Lopez, and Jack Wray playing cards and drinking shots of Southern Comfort. They'd been at it for a while. All three were drunk.

God was the topic of conversation, as usual. Wray was saying he believed in God, while Zayas was saying screw him.

Flores didn't stick around; he took Jessica to the Cutler Ridge Mall, where they roamed around the stores. When they got back home, the card game was still going strong and now, the three were betting on shots. They were squabbling about a range of topics: religion, politics, rap music.

Young Jacob told Flores, in a drunk's whisper, that he was going to "whoop Wray's ass," while Anthony Lopez sat at the table chanting "whoop his ass, whoop his ass." Jacob told Wray they were "going to run a fade," meaning that they were going to fight as they were leaving. Things were tense, but to Flores it appeared to be trash talk; they were joking around.

Meanwhile, Jessica told the police that after they returned from the mall, she was approached by Jacob while Jack Wray was in the bathroom. Jacob told Jessica he was planning on running a one-on-one fade with Wray. When she asked why, Jacob told her that Wray had double-crossed him. Jacob promised her that he would not do this in the house or at the apartment complex out of respect for her, Flores, and the children, and to prevent any problems with them.

By now, it was close to 11:00 p.m. The three were very drunk and they decided to leave the apartment so Wray could call his employer. Jack Wray did not want to drive, so he gave Anthony Lopez his keys. Anthony drove Wray's car with Jacob Zayas seated behind Wray, who rode shotgun. Soon, the three were back at the apartment, and Jacob told Jessica and Feilberto that he would need them to pick him up at Black Point Marina, about two miles away, after the fight.

They agreed; they needed to go to the grocery store for a few essentials, like baby formula, anyway. The three left in Wray's car while the couple drove off to Publix in their car, only to find the Publix was closed. Then the couple drove over to the Marina, as promised.

There in the Black Point Marina parking lot, out of the darkness came Jacob, running, and carrying a bag that he was obviously trying to hide from them. Jumping in the back seat, Jacob told them, "We merked him" and "We yoked him." They knew this meant being killed. Next, Anthony Lopez ran to the car, and now there were flames shooting up in the night. When Anthony got into the car, he smelled like gasoline.

Jacob told the couple, "You all see no evil, you all hear no evil, you didn't think I could do that." He continued by stating coldly that he enjoyed killing Wray, who had "taken my hundred dollars." Anthony Lopez said nothing.

Next, the four drove to Wal-Mart. The couple still had baby formula and things to buy. Jacob and Anthony left them at Wal-Mart to shop, borrowing their car, and later returned to the store to pick them up. Back at the apartment, Jacob threatened Flores that if he said anything to anybody, Jacob would kill his kids. Shortly afterwards, Jacob and Anthony left, ending up in Philadelphia at Jacob's mother's house.

With the information provided by the young couple, Miami police had two prime suspects in the murder of Jack Wray. One quick phone call and within hours, Philadelphia police had arrested both Anthony and Jacob for homicide.

Anthony Lopez told the Philly cops what had happened that night, filling in the gaps to what the Miami police had discovered already. According to Anthony, he had bought the Southern Comfort because both Wray and Zayas were under age; Wray took money out of an ATM and gave it to Anthony to make the purchase. Then they returned to the apartment to drink and play cards.

About a half hour later, Jacob Zayas pulled Anthony aside and told him he wanted to bet Wray that he would give him $50 for drinking the rest of the bottle of Southern Comfort, and while Jack was drinking from the bottle, Jacob wanted Anthony to hit Jack in back of neck with an asp.

Anthony believed that Jacob had some kind of vendetta against Jack Wray, but he knew little more. So after Zayas' request, Anthony came behind Wray and pretended like he was going to hit him, but then stopped and shook his head, indicating to Jacob that he would not go through with it. Zayas nodded his head like he was disappointed. Jack Wray was unaware that any of this was going on behind his back.

They kept drinking, bickering, playing cards. At the next break, Anthony explained that Jacob pulled him aside with another scheme: now, he wanted Anthony to put Wray in handcuffs and put duct tape across his mouth after he'd bet Wray he couldn't down the bottle of whiskey. If Anthony would handcuff and duct tape Jack Wray, "he would do the rest."

Back at the table, although hesitant, Wray ultimately agreed to being handcuffed while chugging the booze. After Wray was handcuffed, Jacob pinched his nose and poured alcohol into Wray's mouth. Anthony wouldn't duct tape the boy. Jack Wray started getting "rowdy" and Anthony uncuffed him.

They kept drinking. Soon, Jacob was back, whispering to Anthony of another "plan." Now, they would convince Jack Wray to leave the house in the car to go purchase marijuana and then while Anthony was driving, Jacob would strangle ("yoke") Jack from the back seat with a cable he had grabbed from the bedroom.

Anthony didn't take Jacob seriously. The three left together purportedly to go buy some marijuana, and Jacob convinced Jack to cover his face so he wouldn't be recognized by the dealer. Jacob sat directly behind Jack, and after Jacob had the mask on, he told Anthony to turn the car lights off. Anthony did so, and soon he heard Jack struggling. He turned the car lights on. Anthony told police he saw that Jacob Zayas had his knee behind the seat, and with his hands crisscrossed he was choking Wray with the cable. Anthony said that he kept telling Jacob to stop, not to do this. He refused to help when Jacob asked him to hold Jack down. Jack Wray did not struggle long.

After Anthony Lopez checked to make sure that Wray was dead, he agreed to burn the car. Then, according to Lopez, he and Jacob ran to where they had seen Jessica and Feilberto pull into the parking lot.

Based on the statement given to the Philadelphia Police Department, the state of Florida indicted Anthony Lopez for first degree premeditated murder and arson. The indictment was shortly followed by its Notice of Intent to Seek the Death Penalty.

I was appointed to represent Anthony Lopez as his lead criminal defense attorney. I would come to learn that Anthony Lopez was a product of a horrible life. His involvement in this horrible crime — with no real motive — brought to light the impact of repeated violence and the slow dissipation of empathy upon a human soul as I had never before seen in my career.

As usual, I put together my defense team and we began to gather background information on Anthony Lopez's upbringing, how he ended up working at a grocery store here in Florida, and what happened in the car that night with Jacob and Jack. Putting together the story of Anthony Lopez was long and difficult for our team; it was a mishmash of facts that we found both here and in Puerto Rico, and the task often proved to be emotionally draining, even over-whelming. Work like this can haunt you.

We learned that Anthony was born on July 7, 1977, in Rio Piedras, Puerto Rico, to a 15-year-old mother and a 26-year-old father. His mother told us that she never knew her father and that her mother, who was a drug addict, died of an overdose when she was only 14 years old. Anthony's mother reported that she was raped at 11 years old and from the moment she met Anthony Lopez, Sr., she realized that he was her only "option."

Anthony's father began to court his mother when she was 13 years old. The following year, she moved in with Anthony Lopez, Sr. and she recalled her first years with him as physically abusive (he would beat her) and emotionally manipulative. He was jealous of their child, and when little Anthony would cry as a baby, he held her down so that she could not pick up the baby.

During the day she would clean houses for a living and Anthony's father would paint houses. He began spending most of his money on booze, so she took her son and moved in with a distant family member. Anthony's father moved back in with his parents. They would move the baby back and forth between them.

When Anthony was four years old, his mother dropped him off with his dad on her way to work; when she returned that evening to pick him up, she was told that Anthony Lopez, Sr., had left Puerto Rico for New York. He had taken the boy with him. She would not see her son for a year, when a distant family member called to tell her where they were in New York and she flew to Manhattan to grab her boy and bring him back to Puerto Rico with her.

By this time, Anthony spoke only English. His mother spoke only Spanish. In a few months, Anthony's father returned to Puerto Rico and once again, he stole his son back to New York. This time, Anthony's mother did not try to retrieve her son.

In New York, Anthony Lopez, Sr., made his living begging for money — panhandling on Manhattan streets. He would take his son with him to help him gain sympathy while he panhandled for money, and Anthony's earliest memory would be begging for money on the streets of New York.

Later, to psychologists, Anthony would remember these years as "a struggle," where all their money went to support his father's drugging and drinking. In an interview with his aunt, she recalled Anthony's father being arrested for panhandling and getting a phone call from the police that "they had a kid." After that, several family members would take in Anthony and his father because "we felt sorry for the kid."

Anthony worshipped his father, and was very protective of him. He remained in denial about many aspects of his childhood, his memories not jiving with the social worker reports we found. He would recall his father was strict about school and "he would beat me if I didn't bring the right books home." He reported that there was always a roof over his head, clean clothes and adequate food.

This was not true, according to the public agency files we reviewed. Police reports showed the two to be homeless; a social worker's report from St. Agatha's dated April 6, 1988, indicated that Anthony and his father "…are very close and protective of each other; corroborating false stories."

The most egregious example of his denial about the truth of his father's abuse was found in hospital records, where we discovered that Anthony had suffered second and third-degree burns that covered approximately 35% of his body. According to Anthony, his father was angry at him and wanted to teach him a lesson, so he poured alcohol on him and set him on fire; afterward, his father told him that if he told anyone what happened, they would take him away. Anthony told hospital staff that he burned himself. The reports indicated that Anthony's father had waited nine days before taking him to the hospital: this behavior is inconsistent with Anthony inflicting his own injuries, but totally consistent with a man trying to avoid criminal charges or the loss of child custody or parental rights.

As a result of the burns, Anthony was in the hospital many months — until his father snuck him out of the hospital and they fled back to Puerto Rico. Anthony was eight years old.

Anthony had no memory of his mother before this — and now, hurt and in pain, he could understand her but was unable to communicate with her in Spanish. He was very sick. Anthony recalled to us "this suit I had to wear for my skin," and how he "…hated to have to get in and out of that suit because it hurt."

He remembered that part of his burn recovery meant that he took medication that made him release his bladder "so I was always wet." His mother discussed this time with her son without much empathy: she described her son as "different." She stated that he did not want to be touched, he wet himself on several occasions, and he was "quiet." When it was pointed out to her that her 8-year-old boy was recovering from severe burns and was likely in great pain, she acknowledged the injury but again replied that "he was still different."

Perhaps the scarring was a problem. Anthony's mother told us that she made an appointment for her son with a plastic surgeon; however, the night before she was supposed to take him to the surgeon, his father took him back to New York once more without telling her. Anthony did not see his mother again until he was sitting in the Miami jail awaiting his murder trial.

Anthony was forced to return with his father by the state of New York under threat of criminal charges against both Anthony Sr. and other family members. Upon his return, Anthony was immediately removed from his father's custody and sent to a group home. The reason cited was child neglect, for his father not taking him to the hospital sooner after the burns. Anthony was placed at St. Agatha's, a residential treatment facility for emotionally disturbed children, ran by the Administration of Children Services and New York Fondling Hospital.

St. Agatha's used treatment teams and focused on the behavioral component aspect of the child. Group cottages were staffed by workers with intense supervision. For the next eight years, Anthony lived the majority of the time at this group home. He reported that he adjusted "pretty okay."

However, reports from the group home indicate that Anthony was very self-conscious about his body because of the scars from the burns. He would defecate on himself and then hide his underwear. He was described as scared and "a loner." Anthony stated that "new, older boys" were admitted to the group home. He stated that he and others were bullied by these boys, and at age 13, Anthony subsequently escaped and went to live with his father.

He said that his father was living with "his new girlfriend in Queens." Anthony reported that both she and his father were drinking heavily. They would often argue and fight. After a few months, Anthony voluntarily returned to the group home.

When asked about sexual abuse while at the group home, Anthony denied any. However, he did recall an incident when he "cursed out" Mr. Dowling, a case manager, and as punishment was made to strip naked and run through the cottage in front of all the other residents. He stated that he was embarrassed, particularly because he was still somewhat self-conscious of the scarring from the burns. Anthony's perspective? "It was effective," he said, "I never cursed at staff again."

A report was filed at the group home in Anthony's name, and an investigation ensued. Nothing came of it. Anthony reported that Mr. Dowling became his mentor and would take him out into the community and "try to teach me things." So much for recognizing abusive behavior.

Records revealed that one of St. Agatha's social workers, Raymond Fernekes, spent a considerable time with Anthony. He described Anthony as a big follower who was not aggressive. According to Fernekes, Anthony would always wear extra clothing to cover his burns. Anthony liked mechanical things, and as a result, Fernekes recommended that he attend a vocational program. St. Agatha's was trying to build a future for Anthony once he turned 18.

Social worker reports from that time indicated that Anthony's father was unable to stop drinking. He would often tell the social worker that he had checked into a treatment center, but it would be a lie. Anthony's father would give them fake information — phony names for treatment centers, made-up street addresses. The boy's only other family support was an aunt, who lived on Staten Island. Anthony was often returned to the group home from visits to her house dirty and unkempt.

According to a report on January 15th, 1991, Anthony's father was "inconsistent." He returned Anthony back to the group home one day late, and then two days late, on two separate overnight visits. He failed to maintain an adequate living situation in that his apartment had no running water and no stove. Additionally, the social workers reported that they often smelled alcohol on Anthony's father's breath. When confronted, he denied it.

On Christmas of 1990, when Anthony was 13 years old, he returned home for the holidays to stay with his father. However, he was returned to the group home by a friend of his father's because "...his father was drinking for five days non-stop. He was admitted to LaGuardia Hospital that night because of delirium tremors." The social worker's report also stated that Anthony was "scared and dirty." Mr. Fernekes, a social worker, wrote "[C]hild needs these visits with father. He feels a sense of concern that father will end up living in the streets or something violent will happen to him."

On November 9, 1990, a judge had ordered that Anthony be sent home at the end of January as long as his father remained in alcohol treatment. However, since housing was inadequate and Anthony's father was unable to remain sober, he was never allowed to reunite with his father.

Reunification was always the goal for Anthony, and Anthony wanted this. However, his father was unable to meet the requirements to regain custody of his son. Anthony said, "I thought I would get out of the group home but then I lost hope. I knew he wouldn't get his act together."

By 17 or 18, Anthony had very little contact with other family members and he had lost complete contact with his father. When he aged out (became a legal adult), he left the group home and reestablished contact with his cousins and aunt in Staten Island. His cousins would tell investigators that Anthony was a follower, loving, never violent, shy, and always respectful.

Having gathered all our background information on Anthony Lopez, it was time for our defense to get expert analysis on what everything we had discovered meant, from a psychological standpoint. Did we have mitigating factors under Florida law? What were they?

I hired psychologist Dr Heather Holmes. Here, in her own words, are Dr. Holmes' clinical impressions as stated in her evaluation:

Mr. Lopez was taken from his mother at a young age. He was stolen by his father, a man who physically abused him and exposed him to poverty, panhandling, and drug use. They were often homeless and Mr. Lopez reported feeling "used." However, his father, although abusive and neglectful, was the single most influential factor in Mr. Lopez's life because he was the only consistent relationship that Mr. Lopez had until he reached adulthood.

Mr. Lopez's lifestyle of being separated from his mother and moving around a lot or being homeless as a child precluded him from forming lasting relationships with others. Instead, it created an enmeshed and mutually dependent relationship with his father. This unhealthy closeness that was formed led to Mr. Lopez choosing to protect his father from the authorities by claiming that he set himself on fire. It also led Mr. Lopez to leave his mother in Puerto Rico to stay with the man who burned him.

According to several reports by social workers from the group home, Mr. Lopez never gave up hope that he would be reunited with his father. He continued to isolate himself from peers and the only relationships he forged were with older men. Arguably, he was eager to please with other men in an attempt to recreate this unhealthy but familiar relationship he had with his father, whom the state of New York forced him to be separated from.

As an adult, Mr. Lopez has continued to seek out closeness with other males. In fact, Mr. Lopez likely sought out other men who were manipulative or unavailable. However, throughout our several meetings together, Mr. Lopez described all of his relationships as him looking up to the other person. He liked learning things such as historical facts or how to lift weights from his friends Jason and

Teddy. He reported thinking that his co-defendant, Jacob, was very smart and detached. These seemed to be qualities that Mr. Lopez admired. Further, he brought a hand-carved chess set and his sketchbooks out for one of our meetings and then remarked that he thought he was meeting with his (male) attorney. When we met on another occasion, Mr. Lopez inquired of the correctional officer who was here to see him and upon discovering that it was this examiner, a female, he elected not to bring out any more sketchbooks or art-work.

Mr. Lopez seems to be unconsciously attempting to re-create the enmeshed and dependent relationship that he had with his father with other males. Therefore, he is emotionally stunted and imma-ture. Given his disinterest in dating and the manner in which he talked about his friends, it is this examiner's opinion that Mr. Lopez is emotionally fourteen or fifteen years of age. Thus, he may look up to boys or men who are younger than him because of the difference between his chronological age and his emotional one. Lastly, Mr. Lopez is eager to please with men that he may look up to.

Anthony would learn that his father died while he was await-ing trial. His aunt from Staten Island traveled to Miami to give him the news face-to-face; according to his aunt, Anthony's response was that "he did not care." Anthony Lopez, Sr. died on June 25, 2000; he was homeless, living on the New York City streets at the time.

Meanwhile, at our offices, we prepared to try Anthony's defense case, fighting for mercy on the basis of Anthony's psychological weaknesses. There were reasons that Anthony didn't do more to stop the death of Jack Wray that night.

On the first day of trial, on a Monday afternoon, the jury panel entered the room and jury selection was scheduled to begin. We stood as the line of people filed into the courtroom to take their seats, Anthony Lopez and I, side by side.

There, at the defense table, Anthony decided to accept a plea of thirty years that we had negotiated with the prosecution earlier. There would be no jury; there would be no trial. It was a smart decision.

Not only would he escape death, or a life sentence, by taking the plea deal, Anthony took an opportunity to have some kind of life on the outside in the future. Anthony Lopez, Jr. remains behind bars at the time of this writing.

Chapter Five:
Bad Company

I GOT THE call on a hot, sunny Thursday afternoon. It was David Brenner, a lawyer I knew only by reputation, and here he was reaching out to me for help — asking that I come on board in a pretty heavy capital murder case because there simply weren't enough death-qualified lawyers over in Fort Myers to handle the appointments. It's true that not all criminal defense lawyers are qualified to handle death penalty cases, and it's a sad fact that many jurisdictions are spread pretty thin when the time comes to appointing death-qualified counsel.

This wasn't the first time I'd had a call like this — and one of the main things I had to weigh was the balance between my Miami practice and the location of the case. Travel time is a burden not only on me, but on my staff and fellow lawyers, who have to help me cover the usual office load when I'm somewhere else. And, of course, there's also the consideration of family time: I'm not home enough as it is, what will taking a case in another part of the state mean to my wife and kids? My wife is a prosecutor, she understands what I do — but my boys are young. They just know that Daddy's gone again. Was David's situation worth the sacrifice?

At first I wasn't very sure, but David just kept talking, and after a long, persuasive conversation he got me to agree to come on board as his co-counsel on this horrible, horrible case.

He's a very good lawyer — he had sold me. David and I now represented Kemar Johnston, who, along with eight other defendants, was facing murder charges. Young lives, essentially over, all because of a birthday party gone bad: yes, *Kemar's* birthday party.

Forging a team
What followed was an uncomfortable, mind-numbing working relationship for the next two years that was always unique and sometimes even reckless. Right out of the gate, let me go on record that David Brenner is undisputedly a genius, and one of the best lawyers I know. He's creative; he thinks outside the box; he's different.

Unfortunately, that creative genius can be stressful and hard to work with — I found that David could be unnerving and in every sense of the word, a very, very hard person with whom to do business. No trial lawyer is easy, granted, but this was a whole new ball game for me. And when it came to the death penalty, we both had to find a way — as co-counsel where our client's life was on the line — to compromise our positions and come together as a cohesive force aimed at doing the right thing for Kemar Johnston, our client.

We locked horns time and time again, fighting to force our way on the other, until we would find compromise. Maybe it made us better lawyers; certainly it made for a better defense, as we meshed our backgrounds and perspectives into finding a way to a defense that was the most effective and efficient. And our client needed everything each one of us could bring to the table.

Kemar Johnston was sitting in a Florida jail, facing the death penalty, when I agreed to come on board as his lawyer. The state had so much evidence it was in the catbird's seat. In many ways, this case was a prosecutor's dream: no wonder Dave and I would periodically clash in frustration.

We were facing two experienced and talented prosecutors. Bob Lee, the senior prosecutor, was a soft-spoken southern gentleman, who could tell a story better than anyone I ever met. I sensed a jury would love him. Just as good was the second prosecutor, Marie Doerr. She was fair, aggressive, and very ethical. Together, they were a formidable team.

The State's Theory
Each side has a theory of the case; that is, how the crime unfolded. The state's theory was two young men were brutally murdered just because they were in the wrong place at the wrong time and mouthed off, after having got themselves in the middle of a drug deal gone bad. And the state attorneys were arguing that our client, Kemar Johnston, pulled the

trigger on both victims. For this, they were taking the position that the sentence of death should be imposed.

Since the crime happened at a huge gathering, there were
lots of people around who saw or heard things relevant to the
case. Dozens and dozens of eyes and ears witnessed the
events that night: no wonder the state was so confident.

Discovery revealed more of what happened: Francisco
and his 14-year-old cousin Luis were not invited to Kemar's
birthday party, but they came anyway and crashed it. Crashing
a party after failing to pay for the drugs you had purchased
was a tragic, foolish mistake for these two boys. Soon, the
two were tied up with shoestrings from a pair of tennis shoes
inside the party house. The partygoers were told "all snitches
leave."

Witnesses recollected that Francisco and Luis were
brought into the kitchen, where they were beaten at first. This
was not enough; later, the two were tortured by two young
girls, one fourteen. The girls carved into the men's backs with
a knife, and then poured bleach and salt on the open wounds.
The bodies revealed that at some point they were also burnt
numerous times with a lighter.

According to the state's theory, Kemar Johnston shot
one of the boys in the house and proceeded to order that
they be taken to Lex Fernandez's car and thrown in the trunk.
Now, the scene — already horrifically ugly — became truly
sinister. Many of the group jumped into multiple vehicles and
in a caravan, transported the boys several miles from the
party location.

There, Francisco and Luis were pulled from the trunk
and executed. Evidence at the kill site revealed that Luis ran

away for a brief moment before he was gunned down. Witness statements told us that later that night, co-defendants Paul and Ant returned to set the car on fire, both bodies in it, attempting to burn the evidence that was left.

Prosecutors were prepared to tell the jury that around 30 young men and women between the ages of 16 and 22 were involved in this horror at some point in time. Either they were inside the house at the time of the beatings and torturing of Francisco and Luis, or they were involved in the discussion regarding if, where, and how to kill them. The state would have psychological expert testimony to support its theory that teen peer pressure, fueled with anger, resentment, and vindication, was a contributing factor to the two homicides.

The prosecution was relying on a number of these witnesses to prove their cases against the defendants: many of the state's witnesses had cut deals, avoiding being charged with crimes themselves (including murder) through their cooperation. We had to take their statements with a grain of salt; these people were trying to save their own skins; they'd have a bias, which meant that much more work for our side.

The Defense Theory

Any defense investigation must happen independently of the state's work — we have to read every document, talk to every person that the prosecution's team does. It's a duplicated effort, sure, but it would be malpractice for any defense lawyer to sit back, trusting and relying on the prosecution's efforts. Surprise, surprise. The state may not perceive the same information as important that we do; in some instances, prosecutors have been known to withhold evidence from the defense. They're not supposed to do this, but overzealous prosecutors have thwarted justice in their zeal to win.

This case was investigation-heavy and we had the alleged triggerman in Kemar. And I was operating on a team located in another town, working to turn over every stone to find all the facts necessary to defend this young man in a death case.

During our own investigation, we talked with everyone at the party that night, as well as following other leads. Our team learned that the state of Florida was going to try and convince the jury that Kemar Johnston deserved to die because of events that started to spiral downward some days before the party started. The time window exponentially expanded — more investigation for us.

Apparently, several days before Kemar's birthday bash, there had been a drug deal between one of the young men living with Kemar, a roommate named Ken Lopez who everyone knew as "Ant." Ant had sold one of the victims, 18-year-old Francisco, some drugs on an I.O.U. In exchange, Francisco promised Ant that if Ant fronted him the drugs, Francisco would bring him the payment later. Francisco reneged; failing to pay would be part of the reason he was so brutally murdered that night, according to the prosecution.

As the case progressed, not only against our defendant but also against his co-defendants, we had the added burden of growing media coverage of the case. Pre-trial publicity escalated after the release of information that Kemar, along with his friends Ant, Cody, Paul, Rod, Ashley, and Melissa, was part of a rap group called "Cash Feenz," which the Cape Coral police ultimately designated as a gang.

Now, the news stories would cover our case as a gang-related killing. The Cash Feenz, according to the police, committed crimes of burglary and violence, and now they had committed the ultimate crime of murder. Kemar Johnston was designated by the police as the "leader" of this so-called gang.

Our concerns regarding the publicity were not unfounded. During the trial, the local and regional news were present daily with TV cameras and microphones. The jurors' appearance on television and the fact that they were put in the awkward position of having to answer to the local community about the outrageous and high publicity charges that were confronting them in this particular case were a big problem for us.

Guilt Phase

From the beginning, David and I agreed that our defense would have to stand on the truth we had gleaned from our own investigation: although Kemar was present during the events that transpired the night of the homicide, his involvement was minimal because of his significant use of Xanax in combination with alcohol and marijuana. You couldn't get to the question of whether or not Kemar was approving of the beatings, torture, or killings; the reality was that Kemar was so high at his birthday party that night that he would have been physically incapable of the acts that the prosecution attributed to him.

David and I came to agree on an integrated defense that was related both to first and second phases of the trial: guilt and penalty. In the first phase, guilt or innocence, we took the position that Kemar was minimally involved and merely present during much of the violence that occurred inside of the house. We believed that Kemar did not leave the house, nor did he go to the kill site where the two young men were ultimately executed. We had evidence that someone who looked very similar to Kemar — his testifying co-defendant, Paul Nunez — was the man who had been identified as Kemar Johnston by witnesses at the kill site.

Paul was one of the defendants who actually had a motive to do the killings, having been ripped off by Francisco, and Paul did resemble Kemar. I had deposed Paul several months before the trial. Paul's deposition wasn't the longest I had ever taken — only 16 or so hours, but it was one of the most intense. The deposition had Bob Lee, his team, and all of the co-defendants' attorneys in attendance. But from the beginning, it was as if no one was in the room except Paul and I. As I probed into Paul's relationships with the other defendants, Paul became less and less reticent. In the end, he was eagerly describing the different types of guns that he had handled and was familiar with. I was sure to bring this fact to the attention of the jury during my cross-examination.

An Unexpected Sidebar

Lex Fernandez appeared on the witness stand, manacled and wearing the bright orange jumpsuit of the incarcerated. Lex had a good lawyer I knew from Fort Myers, Kevin Shirley. Kevin negotiated a plea deal for Lex to get 26 years in prison in exchange for testifying against Kemar and Ant.

I needed to show the jury that it was Lex who was a killer, a cold and callous individual who witnesses said had stepped over the tied bodies of Francisco and Luis there in the kitchen as he got some more booze. The jury had to see that Lex was only testifying to get a reduced sentence, not out of a desire to tell the truth.

Cross-examination is an art unto itself. It takes years to perfect getting the witness on the "yes train." You start by asking non-confrontational questions that the witness agrees with. "You are presently in jail, aren't you?" "Yes." "You went to the party, didn't you?" "Yes." The questions gradually build in intensity and rapidity until the witness answers instinctively with the truth.

This is where I had Lex Fernandez when I asked him about what his attorney had told him he would get in exchange for testifying against my client, Kemar. No sooner had the question left my mouth than a resounding "Objection!" came from behind me. It didn't sound like Bob Lee; in fact, a puzzled Bob Lee, sitting at the prosecutor's table, swung his chair around to face the crowded benches behind the bar. Standing in the back of the courtroom packed with spectators and TV cameras was Kevin Shirley, Lex's attorney, who added a belated "Your Honor" to his shouted objection.

I always suspected that death penalty attorneys are somewhat of a special breed of attorney, maybe a little bit more passionate than most. Now, Kevin Shirley proved my hypothesis correct. It isn't exactly the usual courtroom pro-

cedure for courtroom spectators to jump up in the middle of
a trial and object to the proceedings.

But the presiding judge, Judge Thomas Reese, took the
interruption in stride and allowed Kevin to come sidebar.
Kevin, Bob Lee, and I approached the bench, and the white
noise generator was flipped on so the jury wouldn't hear the
conversation. Kevin argued that my questions violated attor-
ney-client privilege. His argument was good enough that I
had to rephrase my cross on this point very carefully, and
Judge Reese let him return to the other side of the bar without a word of reprimand.

The Closer

I faced the jury to give one of the most challenging closing
arguments of my career. I was fighting media coverage, the
horrors of the underlying crimes, and the fact that these
jurors already believed Kemar Johnston had kidnapped and
killed Francisco and Luis. How to sway them to save Kemar
from a sentence of death?

I began by discussing how the jury not only had great
responsibility in having to deal with the life and death of
Kemar Johnston, but also having to answer to a community
that was outraged, and should have been outraged, by what
had happened on the night of October 6, 2006. It would their
job to be fair — and this would be hard to do.

Next, I focused on a number of things, one of which was
that the nine witnesses who testified at trial had given thousands of pages of depositions and testimony to police — and
in those thousands of pages, there were hundreds of incon-

sistencies. Things didn't add up between the stories various witnesses told, and you could find inconsistent statements when comparing witness statements made by the same witness, at different times. It was a party; people were high on drugs and emotion; later, they were afraid of being busted: how much could their recollections be trusted as accurate?

I also focused on forensic evidence that was inconsistent with the state's theory. One big schism: there was something hinky about the evidence on how Luis had died, and if he was alive at the time the fire had been set.

My theory of the case (which to this day I believe is consistent with the evidence) was that Paul and Ant were dealing drugs out of Kemar's house in the weeks leading up the homicide. They had an existing, albeit rocky, relationship with Francisco, who was known in the community as a volatile young man who had issues with drugs and alcohol. Francisco also had a reputation for being violent and for carrying a gun. A few weeks before his death, Francisco had gone to Kemar's house and there had been an altercation between Francisco, Paul, and Ant. It was after that squabble that Francisco had returned to Kemar's place to buy the crack cocaine on an I.O.U. from Ant, who was the only one at the house who sold cocaine.

Not that Kemar didn't sell drugs, I told the jury. Kemar dealt marijuana — but only marijuana — he never dealt cocaine or crack-based products. In the drug business, everyone has his own product line, dependent upon his own suppliers and network of buyers. Kemar was a pot dealer.

After Francisco didn't come back with the money he owed Ant for the coke, there was evidence of communica-

tions between Francisco, Ant, and Paul — long before
Francisco showed up at the birthday party. Ant was mad.
Things were unpleasant between them. Two days before the
party, Francisco showed up at Paul's house in the early
morning hours, strung out, wanting some drugs that Ant had
promised him. Francisco got violent when Paul refused to
give Francisco anything, since Ant already waited for payment
on drugs Francisco had already purchased. Angry, Francisco
threw a brick through the windshield of Paul's mother's car
and, yelling, threatened both Paul and Ant. Kemar didn't
have something against the victims, I told the jury: the trouble had been brewing between Francisco, Paul, and Ant over
coke buys.

When it came time for Kemar's birthday party, Paul rode
over to Kemar's place with Ant and Rod, another codefendant. Paul, as usual, carried his 44 Magnum. I reminded the
jury of testimony which showed Paul had a longstanding love
of weapons, having handled approximately 12-14 different
types of weapons, including multiple handguns, rifles and
semi-automatic weapons, by the time he turned 18 years old,
many of which he had fired on the street or through some
target practice at a firing range.

I took the jury through what we knew happened that
night. Upon their arrival at the party, Paul, Rod and Ant proceeded to get high on an assortment of drugs and booze. By
the end of the night, they were pretty messed up. My theory
was that when Francisco crashed the party with his cousin
Luis, a belligerent and bombed Paul, Ant, and Rod confronted him — and it was these three who orchestrated the
process of these young men being tied up, tortured, and ulti-

mately murdered. This made sense: they had a reason to be this incensed. Kemar didn't. Kemar was busy getting wasted that night, celebrating his 20th birthday.

And what about codefendant Lex Fernandez, I asked them? I believed Lex Fernandez was one of the shooters, as well as being the driver of the car that held the victims on their way to the kill site. After all, we knew from the evidence that the morning after the party, Lex woke up at Kemar's place, and as he drove back home, found one of the handguns used in the homicide in his glove box. This was in addition to the blood evidence in his trunk.

I also argued that the members of the Cash Feenz group, the rap group that was pilloried in the press as gangster and gang-oriented, were just a couple of young kids trying to make something of themselves in the music industry. I made an analogy between the longhairs who grew up in the 60s and 70s listening to the demon music rock and roll, and to the young of the 50s, when Elvis was scandalized for shaking his hips on the Ed Sullivan Show. Sometimes, the older generation vilifies new musicians, but it doesn't mean they are inherently wicked.

At the end of the guilt portion of the trial, the jury was out for several hours. They returned with a verdict of guilty for both first degree murder and kidnapping. The penalty phase was set the following week.

That closing was long, and it was exhausting. However, we knew that we had substantial mitigation that weighed heavily against even those most heinous of aggravating circumstances.

But because the jury took so long to deliberate, I suspected we also had lingering doubt on our side. Everyone
knows that guilt in a criminal trial must be proven "beyond a
reasonable doubt." But that doesn't mean beyond *any* doubt.
There usually is some amount of doubt — lingering doubt —
that stays with some of the jurors after a guilty verdict. Many
jurors do not feel comfortable sentencing someone to death
— the most final of punishments — if there is any lingering
doubt from the guilt phase. After all, there are no do-overs if
a person is executed. Lingering doubt could prevent a death
sentence in the penalty phase, which was set to begin the next
week.

Kemar's Road to Perdition

I knew our mitigation specialist, Rosalie Bolin, by reputation
as a dedicated and passionate investigator with an uncanny
knack for bonding with people. This was my first time working with Rosalie, but it wouldn't be my last. During Kemar's
trial, I received a call from Rick Sichta, a prominent
Jacksonville attorney, asking me to join him and Rosalie in
the trial of the Dubose brothers, but that story is for another
time.

What should have been a straightforward mitigation
exercise turned out to be quite complicated because neither
Kemar nor his family were willing to accept that Kemar
might be convicted. As a result, they refused to supply
Rosalie with basic information about Kemar's life and the
family.

We only had a very sketchy history to begin with. Born in Saint Mary Parish, Jamaica, Kemar had come with his family to Cape Coral, Florida, when he was about three or four years old. Cape Coral is a small bedroom community historically known as a retirement Mecca, but over the years it has become more popular with middle-class working families. It's not known as a high crime area, like the neighborhoods where many of my clients and their families reside.

Until he was a teenager, Kemar lived with his brother in his father's Cape Coral home. While his father did the best he could, Kemar eventually became uncontrollable — disrespecting authority, hanging out with his friends, smoking pot, and partying hard. Father and son clashed, and Kemar left home while he was still a teenager. Kemar had lots of friends and he preferred them to his family home. Soon he was sharing a place with several buddies; it would prove to be a tragic and life-altering mistake.

Kemar's cousin finally tipped Rosalie that Kemar's mother could be found selling trinkets under a clock in Kingston, Jamaica. That was all the information she had when she and I took off to Jamaica on what I was convinced was a wild goose chase. I'm not a pessimist, but Kingston is a pretty big place.

Jamaica is beautiful, especially if you are a tourist and can stay in the lovely Hilton we checked into. For anyone thinking of becoming a mitigation specialist, a warning: While you may travel to glamorous places, your job will more often than not take you to the underbelly that tourists never see. Our driver was also our bodyguard as we plunged into the heart of Kingston to find Kemar's mother.

Fortunately, the driver knew the market under the clock tower. Undaunted by the bustling crowd, Rosalie queried street vendor after street vendor until we were directed to the spot where Kemar's mother habitually set up shop. Rosalie and I staked out the spot until a woman whom Kemar resembled started setting out her wares — little hairbrushes, umbrellas, anything for under a dollar. Kemar's mother was at first unwilling to talk to her, wanting money in exchange for information.

Rosalie was determined to travel in Kemar's footsteps to all the places significant in his young life. This voyage led us up unpaved roads into the mountainous Jamaican rain forest. Our driver wisely only traveled during daylight; the road had no guardrails to prevent a car from slipping over the cliffs. Rosalie began to think of this as the road to perdition.

When we finally reached Saint Mary's Parish and Kemar's grandmother, we were greeted by a simplicity and innocence that we hadn't expected amid the deprivation and poverty. Kemar's old schoolyard was unchanged since he had been there; children dressed in crisp uniforms and carried outdated torn textbooks. I think the children got to Rosalie and me the most. She brought out a video camera, and the children shyly approached. She asked them if they would sing a song for Kemar, a Jamaican boy from their school who was in bad trouble. Spontaneously, the children began to sing the Jamaican national anthem. Our driver straightened and removed his hat, his hand hastily wiping the tears from the corners of his eyes. He wasn't alone.

Rosalie found mitigation and records I didn't think could be found. I still have memories of her digging through thousands of dusty hospital records, which were bundled with string into stacks. No index, no filing system, just a random order. Somehow she found the one tattered piece of paper documenting Kemar's head injuries that he suffered falling from the schoolyard wall. Her determination even got us into a stiffly formal and ultimately futile interview with Jamaica's Secretary of Agriculture in an attempt to find out if ganja spraying had put toxins into the environment of Saint Mary's Parish.

During penalty phase, David did a brilliant job of presenting Kemar's life to the jury using a powerful and moving Powerpoint presentation that Rosalie compiled. David called a number of very well-known experts, establishing that Kemar was under the influence of Xanax, marijuana, and alcohol that night. He also put on evidence that Kemar suffered from frontal lobe brain damage, as well as evidence that Kemar had suffered abuse and neglect throughout his childhood, first in Jamaica and later in Florida, while living with his father. David gave the jury evidence that at the time of this homicide, Kemar's brain was not functioning in a way that is consistent with someone who knows the consequences of their actions.

David argued that on the scales of justice, Kemar should not die. Maybe that could not be said for some of his codefendants, but Kemar Johnston should be spared.

Fortunately, the jury agreed. They returned a recommendation of life imprisonment, which was a victory for both Kemar Johnston and his family. Kemar remains incarcerated today.

Chapter Six:
The Lost Soul

MIAMI IS A spicy mix of cultures and people from all over
the world. Particularly rich is its Cuban heritage — a heritage
that also brings with it the old religion known as Santeria.
Santeria came to Florida via Cuba and has its origins in
Africa. It is a religion that carries with it Catholic symbolism
as well as reliance upon a purported power of magical spells
to manipulate the lives of both its followers and the people
surrounding them.

To most people outside of South Florida, their only
exposure to Santeria is maybe the old Desi Arnaz song
"Babalu" from reruns of "I Love Lucy." But in certain parts
of Miami on certain nights, you can hear the drum lines. A
tourist straying only a block or two off picturesque Calle
Ocho may be puzzled by stores advertising their wares as
"Botanica y Pet Store."

As an attorney, Santeria is very real to some of my clients. Visit the Miami Dade criminal courthouse on any given morning, and a careful observer may first smell, then see, a paper bag marked "Pollo" containing a dead chicken. Families would leave these and other relics as offerings around the courthouse in the hope of a favorable legal outcome for a loved one. Rumor has it that the courthouse has its janitors patrol the outside of the building early in the morning and remove these decaying items before the daily onslaught of employees, judges, and jurors arrive.

And, as I soon found out, Santeria played a very important role for Henry Cuesta, my newest client.

A Good Catholic Boy

As a parent, sometimes I just sit at my desk and shake my head, asking myself, "How in the hell did this guy get to the point of doing a horrible crime like this, when he had all the advantages and two loving, caring, and protective parents?" Most of my clients face the death penalty, and most of them come to me with histories of extreme poverty, abuse, neglect, lack of education — the kinds of backgrounds that most of us expect these folk to have. Not Henry Cuesta. Henry was one of those clients that puzzled me as a parent — what more could they have done?

Henry's mom and dad were devout Catholics and they raised their children in the church. Henry was an altar boy, raised in a comfortable home in suburban South Florida. His kid brother Ignacio was a college graduate with a good job and a promising future. Looking at this family from the

outside, not in a million years would I have thought that a
child from this home would have his name on a file setting
on my desk, as he stood accused by the state of Florida of
committing an extremely cold and callous assassination.

Henry was born on March 8, 1973, to Armando and
Martha Cuesta. His childhood home was filled with religious
statutes, crucifixes, and other symbols of Catholicism; spiritu-
ality played a consistent part of his childhood. The Cuesta
family was (and is) close; Henry, his parents, and his brother
have always shared a bond.

Growing up, Henry had saved someone's life on two different occasions. When Henry was eight years old, he jumped
into a pool to save a baby that had fallen into the water.
When he was 17 years old, while fishing with Ignacio, he
helped rescue someone from drowning. As a boy, Henry had
been a hero.

Henry did struggle in school; he had problems with his
attention span and a lack of concentration. It was a learning
disability; school records show that Henry never had a
behavioral problem. After his high school graduation, Henry
held various jobs. He wasn't college material.

Right out of high school, Henry married. There was one
child born of the marriage before the two divorced. Henry's
marriage didn't last long.

After the divorce, Henry struggled to hold on to any
form of employment. He became reclusive and began to self-
medicate an undiagnosed mental deterioration with drugs like
Quaaludes, mescaline, acid, rohypnol, cocaine, and marijuana.
This was the backstory that I learned existed when Henry
Cuesta's path crossed with destruction.

A Priest is Murdered

The murder itself happened on April 3, 1998, in a nice, middle-class home located on SW 13th Street in Miami. Dulce Diaz and Jorge Herrera lived and worked out of this house, making a living by leading spiritual readings and conducting rituals that included animal sacrifice. They marketed their services through a local newspaper, and made enough money on their activities to live a nice lifestyle without having to hold any other form of employment.

On that early spring day, a gunman entered their home and shot the couple, leaving them both for dead. Nevertheless, Herrera survived and was able to tell police investigators that the killer had come to the house for a spiritual reading. There were no other witnesses to the shooting and forensic efforts found no additional evidence at the scene: no firearms, no physical evidence, nothing that would help them find the perpetrator. Herrera's recollection, as the sole witness, was the only lead they had.

In situations like this, where there is scant evidence at the scene, the police turn to family and friends of the victim for more information. Usually someone will know something that helps investigators, and in this case law enforcement soon focused the investigation around Dulce's ex-husband, Eusebio Hernandez.

From Dulce's 18-year-old son Isbet, the police had learned bad blood existed between Dulce, Jorge, and Dulce's ex-husband. Isbet explained Eusebio believed Dulce owed him $10,000: money that came from the sale of a property they had owned together. Instead of paying Eusebio his share, Dulce took all the sales proceeds and use the funds as a down payment on the house that she shared with Jorge Herrera, the home where she died. Eusebio was always harassing Dulce about the money.

Police discovered Eusebio was a palero, a priest in the Palo Mayombe religion. Just like Dulce and Jorge, Eusebio made his living by doing spiritual readings. Palo Mayombe is known to most South Floridians; along with Santeria, it is a known religion among local criminal law professionals because many followers of Palo Mayombe are traffickers in illegal drugs.

Many drug traffickers believe Palo Mayombe will provide spiritual protection for them in their dangerous endeavors, mostly through spells and other rituals. Palo Mayombe deals with black magic and the practice of evil, darkness, and the spirits of the dead. A practitioner of the Palo Mayombe religion believes that he can control the soul or spirit of a dead person, and have it do deeds for him or protect him from harm. Palo followers look to spirits manifesting themselves in man and in the forces of nature; worship is done with sacred herbs, sticks (palos), and bones.

Soon, police would discover a connection between the Palo Mayombe priest and my client, the Catholic altar boy Henry Cuesta. While reviewing Dulce's phone records, investigators discovered several calls to and from Daned Loredo, Henry Cuesta's girlfriend. After Ms. Loredo's family had retained counsel and then only under subpoena, young Daned admitted that two days after the shootings, long before the police came around, her boyfriend had told her he was paid $6000 for his part in a drug deal, "...that it went bad, that the guy took out a gun on him, that he shot the guy and the lady came out screaming and he shot her." Miami police brought Henry Cuesta in for questioning.

Twenty-one days after the crime, on April 24, 1998, Henry Cuesta sat with Miami police detectives and told them a very different story. According to Henry, he knew Eusebio Hernandez; they had met through Eusebio's son Anthony, a paraplegic. Henry and Anthony were part of a car club, where a group of young men, all in their early twenties, all sharing a keen interest in special automobiles, would meet to talk cars in front of Anthony's house. They would park their cars in front of the house and work on their vehicles, and they would hang out in the house with Anthony, trading car stories. Eusebio would drop by during car club meetings, being friendly with the young men.

It was here, at the car club, that Eusebio found an easy mark in Henry Cuesta. Henry was unemployed, he lived at home, and he was driving his girlfriend's car. Henry didn't seem to be able to hold a steady job and he was using a variety of narcotics regularly. Prey.

Henry told the police that Eusebio approached him about making some serious money during one of Henry's visits with Anthony: Eusebio said he needed two people killed. Henry's first response was to decline, and he told the Palo priest that he didn't think he could kill somebody. Like any savvy predator, Eusebio persisted. Finally, Henry agreed to Eusebio's request.

After the agreement, according to Henry, came the rituals. Eusebio required Henry to participate in several Palo practices prior to the shooting: there were animal sacrifices, candles were lit, and Henry had to wear certain beads. The priest told Henry after each ritual, "with what I did to you, you ain't gonna have any problems at all, everything should go good." Henry described one ritual in his statement:

> *That same day when I was there, he just did that with the chicken and then with the candles. He was saying something in a language I didn't understand and just the thing with the candles and the chickens. I couldn't turn back to look. He told me to keep looking straight, if not, whatever it was that he said about the religion, that it will go bad, whatever. He just told me to keep looking straight, not to look back.*

Henry told police that Eusebio provided the weapon, the car to drive, and the plan to carry out the killing. Eusebio's plan was for Henry to schedule a spiritual reading with Dulce and Jorge using a false name; once inside the house, Henry could carry out the shootings.

On the day of the shooting, Henry told the cops he met with Eusebio, was given a car, the gun and of course, some rituals were conducted, including placing items in Henry's pocket. Henry couldn't do it; he went to the spiritual reading, but could not kill them. Eusebio was disappointed. Soon, there were more rituals for Henry, and more persuasion. Henry was sent back again, and this time he carried out the shooting.

Mitigation

Based primarily upon Henry's statement, he was indicted along with Eusebio and charged with first degree murder, conspiracy to commit first degree murder, and attempted murder. Now long afterwards, I was appointed as Henry's defense counsel.

Our legal team immediately began researching everything we could learn about our client, and suddenly we entered a world that we would all have preferred to avoid. Not satisfied with his life, and not getting the answers he wanted from his Catholic upbringing, Henry had become involved in Santeria.

Santeria believers carefully follow highly stylized rights of worship: hundreds of herbs are categorized for use in spells and cures, together with stones, seashells, water, and sacrifice. Sacrifice ranges from a few pieces of fruit to money tucked into a tureen, a glass of wine, or a ritualistic death of an animal. The Santerians believe that no favor can be disbursed; no venture begun with hope of success; no daily life lived without sacrifice to soothe the Santerian saints so they will smooth life's passage.

Henry found himself divorced, unable to hold a job, unable to keep a girlfriend, and building failure upon failure. This was not the norm for where Henry came from; he felt pressure to succeed, to do something with his life that my clients coming from the barrio might not experience. Nothing was working, and Henry began turning to drugs — and we learned, de-compensating sometimes into an apparent psychosis state. It was in this environment that Henry learned of Santeria.

His path crossed with a santero (Santerian priest), who began to offer light to Henry that he could see in no other part of his life. It was in this vulnerable state that Henry Cuesta was introduced to Eusebio Hernandez.

As a palero, Eusebio Hernandez was experienced in the
Palo Mayombe rituals that researchers compare to Brazilian
and South American "hex" rituals, originating in a voodoo
counterpart. These rituals essentially brainwash the subjects
into doing things or believing things that manifest themselves
in both physical and psychological reactions. There are
numerous documented examples where people were told they
were going to die because a spell had been cast upon them
and they actually died because of "the spell." It's a honed
practice that goes far from the Las Vegas hypnotist's stage
act, where audience members are hypnotized into squawking
like a chicken. Here, hex rituals are used for dark and sinister
motivations.

When Eusebio Hernandez met Henry Cuesta, he found a
dysfunctional, unusual thinking, troubled young man who
had a serious drug problem. Like any good predator, Eusebio
took advantage of this troubled young man who he knew had
flocked to the rituals of Santeria in order to search for
answers in his life. It was only a small step to take Henry
from Santeria to Palo.

Because Henry's heavy substance abuse essentially
caused him to de-compensate into a psychosis, he was
exceedingly malleable as a target for Eusebio's manipulations.
The key for our defense was to get psychological expertise to
explain the extent of Henry's mental illness — and how this
young man could be controlled in this way.

Henry was evaluated by top-flight experts for the
defense and state. First, Dr. Enrique Suarez evaluated the
defendant on behalf of the state of Florida, finding:

When asked about substance abuse, Mr. Cuesta states that he began drinking beer, liquor or "whatever I could get my hands on" when he was 15 years old. He states that he also began smoking marijuana approximately two times per week during this same time period. He relates that at the age of 17 he began to use an unspecified inhalant ("rush") as well as mescaline (a hallucinogen). Moreover, he states that he was also using pharmaceutical drugs such as quaaludes, in addition to alcohol and marijuana, which he was using more frequently. Mr. Cuesta states that between the ages of 18 and 19, he began using a wide variety of hallucinogenic substances, including LSD and psilocybin mushrooms, on a monthly basis. He states that between the ages of 20 and 22 years old, his consumption of alcohol decreased to an occasional basis. He states, however, that after his divorce in 1995, his drug and alcohol abuse escalated. He states that, up to the time of his arrest, he was using ecstasy (methylphenidate), "roofies" (Rohypnol) and the powdered form of cocaine, three to four times per week, in addition to his continuing use of marijuana and alcohol. Mr. Cuesta denied ever receiving any form of substance abuse treatment. Mr. Cuesta contributed that his family members, with the exception of his brother, were never aware that he was abusing drugs. He added that, although his brother knew he used drugs, he was not aware of the extent of his abuse.

Furthermore, when discussing his medical history Dr. Suarez discovered:

When questioned about head trauma, Mr. Cuesta cited two instances. He contributed that when he was approximately 10 years old, he was hit with a rock on the top of his head. He denies experiencing any loss of consciousness or receiving any type of medical treatment. He states that when he was in the 10th grade he was again hit on the top of the head with a desk. He denies experiencing any loss of consciousness and relates that he was treated at Miami Children's Hospital. He states that he was released after several hours. When questioned about his medical history, Mr. Cuesta denied any medical illnesses, episodes of unconsciousness, seizures or convulsions. He contributed that since 1995, he has suffered from frequent headaches. He indicated that he has continued to have headaches. He indicated that he has continued to have headaches while incarcerated, and notes that approximately one week ago, he was given medications for "cluster headaches." He added that, at times, he experiences blurred vision in conjunction with his headaches.

For the defense, Dr. Herrera also evaluated Henry:

The results obtained by Mr. Cuesta in this neuropsychological evaluation point to the presence of cerebral dysfunction affecting primarily the frontal lobes. In the presence of at least an average level of intelligence, Mr. Cuesta has significant difficulties with executive functions that regulate behavior mediated through the frontal lobes. He also has a marked tendency towards perseveration, or the inability to shift attention adaptively in response to stimulus demands.

The neuropsychological evaluation conducted with this patient points to the presence of someone whose ability to discern the potentially harmful nature of his actions is impaired. He would have difficulties foreseeing the consequences of his actions above and beyond an immediate set of circumstances. The findings obtained in this evaluation also suggest that Mr. Cuesta would be someone who would be easily led, as is apparent in his involvement with Santeria rituals. Mr. Cuesta can also be easily influenced and may be readily led into the wrong path and acquiesce into doing things for others, without being able to foresee the remote consequences of his behavior.

In terms of a diagnostic consideration for this patient, the diagnosis of ICD of 292.82 (drug induced dementia) is estimated to be appropriate. In summary, Henry suffers from frontal lobe drug induced dementia, documented both by history and independent testing.

Before meeting his Svengali, Eusebio Hernandez, our client had exhibited no antisocial behavior; he never been arrested; and he had never received any psychological testing nor any mental health treatment.

After both sides had heard from our experts, I sat down with the state's prosecutor. We hammered out a deal: Henry would go to trial, but I succeeded in convincing the prosecutor to waive the death penalty.

The state's case essentially rested on two prongs: Henry's 60-page confession, and a witness identification by Jorge Herrera, who had survived the shooting. At trial, Elizabeth, my trial partner, and I argued that Henry's 60-page confession was a false confession. This failed, and the lengthy statement was admitted.

Henry's statement going into evidence made dealing with Jorge's testimony all the more important. Saying that Jorge was uncooperative as a witness is an understatement.

Besides being Dulce's significant other, Jorge Herrera
was a "babalawo," or high priest. Both he and Dulce made
significant money from their backyard Santeria practice in the
little shed behind their well-to-do home. Jorge, a slim, athletic
man with chiseled features, was reluctant to answer questions
about the financial aspects of their business. Most unnerving
was his penetrating stare. He focused on me with dark eyes
full of contempt and hatred for someone defending Dulce's
professed killer. I pushed thoughts of a prosecutor who had
awakened to find unwelcome surprises on his doorstep after
convicting a babalawo from my mind.

My cross-examination of him lasted several hours, and
although I am not superstitious, that night at home my lights
flickered at my house for most of the evening. It could have
been the weather, but after studying the occult and voodoo
during the months leading up to the trial, I became convinced
that perhaps I had asked Jorge one too many questions.

Ultimately, Henry Cuesta was convicted and sentenced
by the jury to life in prison without parole. His parents visit
him regularly.

Chapter Seven:
A Child Is Missing

IT IS LATE summer 2008 in Orlando, Florida. Much of the nation is riveted on the search for a beautiful two-year-old girl named Caylee, who has vanished under mysterious circumstances. The mother, a twenty-three-year-old girl herself, did not report her baby missing for nearly 30 days, and the media is whipped into a frenzy with pictures of the attractive young mother partying and dancing during that time.

The excitement and news about the case was barely on my radar screen. I had just finished the death penalty trial of Wadada Delhall and was in the middle of another murder trial. The exhaustion and stress from trying murder cases leaves little time for watching news, even news as dramatic as the arrest of the two-year-old's mother for first degree murder.

When you are in a criminal trial in Miami Dade, all recesses inevitably lead to the courthouse's local restaurant, affectionately known to the long timers as the "Pickle Barrel." I was taking one of these interludes in the Pickle Barrel during the murder trial of Gerard Williams, an armed robbery gone bad, when my phone rang and displayed the caller ID of Mike Walsh.

Mike Walsh is an old friend and happens to be a highly respected criminal defense attorney in Miami. Once we had even been partners and shared an office in nearby tony Coral Gables. But those times were long gone and it had been a while since Mike and I had talked. I answered his call immediately.

Mike's conversation quickly captured my attention. He wanted to make a professional introduction to a friend that once had been our Westlaw sales representative. Mike explained that the recently admitted attorney, Jose Baez, had a new client, and there were rumblings that the state was going to file a death notice. The client? Casey Anthony, the missing two-year-old's mother. Now, the case was on my radar.

Mike set up the call between Jose and me. Jose wanted to talk to me because Mike had made him aware of my extensive death penalty experience and trial expertise. Jose, barely admitted to the Florida bar for three years, was concerned that he might not be allowed to manage the case because he was not qualified to handle a death penalty case in Florida.

Attorney Death Qualification
Florida, like most states with a death penalty, has strict requirements for attorneys who represent defendants that are

facing the death penalty. In fact, any case is considered a capital case if death is a possibility and there has been no formal waiver by the state of its intention to seek the death penalty.

Two lawyers are required since capital trials consist of two separate phases: the guilt phase and the penalty phase. After a defendant is found guilty of a capital offense subject to the death penalty, a second penalty phase trial determines whether death will be imposed. Florida Rule of Criminal Procedure 3.112 lays out the minimum requirements for the two attorneys, known as the lead counsel and the co-counsel.

The qualifications for lead counsel are much higher than those for co-counsel. In addition to being admitted *pro hac vice* or members of the bar in good standing, lead counsel needs at least five years of criminal trial experience. Because the penalty is so serious in a capital case, you had to have tried at least nine trials to completion — plea deals and mistrials don't count. At least two of those trials have to be death penalty trials. In addition, at least three of those nine cases have to be murder cases, or one murder case and five felony trials.

Because the penalty phase determines life and death, lead counsel is required to be experienced "in the utilization of expert witnesses and evidence, including but not limited to psychiatric and forensic evidence; and have demonstrated the necessary proficiency and commitment which exemplify the quality of representation appropriate to capital cases, including but not limited to the investigation and presentation of evidence in mitigation of the death penalty."

The law, like anything else, changes over time. The rule requires that both lead counsel and co-counsel be current and up-to-date in their legal education. At least twelve hours of classes devoted to capital criminal defense within the last two years is required for both attorneys.

The requirements for co-counsel are only slightly less stringent. In addition to the continuing legal education and bar admission, co-counsel needs prior experience in at least three complex jury trials that went to completion. At least two of these were murder trials, or at least one was a murder trial and another a felony.

At this point, I knew little of Jose except for my passing meetings with him when he was selling Westlaw. Jose, while a promising new attorney, did not meet the qualifications for lead counsel. Admitted to practice law in Florida on September 22, 2005, he barely met the three year time requirement for co-counsel. I did not know if he met all the other requirements for co-counsel on a death case, but from the brief phone call, I was convinced that he wanted to do what was best for his client by getting death-qualified lead counsel on the team.

Preemptive Strike

It's odd how some clients will stick with you for years afterward. As I considered Jose's phone call, I could not shake thoughts of another young mother that I had defended. The face of Yvette Yallico, the young girl/mother who heard voices commanding her to drown her daughter, would sometimes pop into my mind as I worked on this very different case. At the time, different facts — a drowned daughter in one, a missing daughter in the other. I had saved Yvette's life; maybe I could do the same for this young woman.

Jose wanted to forestall the filing of a death notice in this case. Even though every first degree murder is technically a capital case, the state is still required to give notice that they plan to seek the ultimate penalty. In Casey's case, the state had not yet filed such a notice. I explained that a waiver package was necessary to convince the state not to file. The waiver package would be a preemptive strike. I agreed to join the team for the specific purpose of a waiver, leaving the issue of who was technically lead counsel open for the time being. Jose and I quickly came to terms on my fee, and I was on board.

I had just finished a short two-day murder trial and had plans to spend time with my family, but I rearranged my schedule and caught a flight to Orlando early Saturday morning. The airport was packed with the usual number of Mickey Mouse ears and Tinkerbell wings perched precariously upon exhausted children departing the magic of Orlando. I must have stood out from the crowd of eager new arrivals — a solitary suited figure with briefcase and cell phone in hand — because Jose quickly pulled up to the curb next to me as I exited the airport. I recognized him almost immediately, threw my briefcase in the car, and we were on our way.

After the brief preliminary "good to see you again," conversation quickly turned to the client. From my research, I knew that our client was being subjected to endless, almost inevitably negative, media attention. Florida's Sunshine Laws allow public access to all manner of information, including the discovery in a criminal case, jail tape recordings, you name

it. The tiniest detail did not escape the attention of the dog-
ged reporters of her case.

Jose was very concerned that all media contact be done
through his public relations agent, the soon to be infamous
Todd Black. Jose warned me that when we visited Casey in
jail, my name would be on the sign-in ledger and to expect
my involvement to become public.

If you have never visited someone in jail, strict security
measures are followed. All visitors must log into a ledger
before passing through a metal detector. Orlando was the
same, but the guards seemed to recognize Jose, and we were
quickly escorted to a cement block room that doubled as an
inmate classroom to meet Casey. Jose and I sat side-by-side in
plastic chairs at a table, silently waiting for our client to be
brought in.

A female guard soon arrived with a young woman
dressed in a jail jumpsuit. From the news coverage, I recognized her as Casey — but it was hard to reconcile this fright-
ened young woman with the images plastered across the
internet and television. Gone was the makeup and the wild
animation shown in those pictures. She seemed like more of a
child with a scrunchy ponytail pulling her hair from her face,
exaggerating the size of her eyes. Her gaze focused immediately on Jose, and she smiled.

Casey sat across from us, and the guard left the room,
closing the door but staying in the corridor outside, should
help be needed. I sensed that Casey very much viewed Jose as
her protector. Jose briefly touched her hand in greeting, and
introduced me as the attorney he had told her about who
would explain about the death penalty.

It is always unnerving to a client and their family to have to consider the possibility of an execution. I always try to reassure them first that I have the right experience, and then gently begin to walk them through the process. I explained to Casey that my job was not to defend her innocence or guilt — that was in Jose's hands, not mine. Instead, my job was to understand her as a unique person. At this point, she did not need to talk to me about her case, but just about her life. I explained that that I would be meeting with her family and friends as well as her, and we would just talk about things important to her.

My theory has always been that jurors, even those who are willing to follow the law and vote for death, are reluctant to kill someone once they begin to view them as flawed, but fellow human beings. This is why I wanted to learn about her life in order to present Casey to the jury if it ever came to a penalty phase proceeding.

Casey expressionlessly accepted my explanation. Because I needed to meet Casey's parents, George and Cindy Anthony, later that day, we drew the meeting to a close with a promise that I would be returning next week to meet with her again. Jose signaled the guard, who unlocked the door. Casey walked to the door of the room with us. Jose and I turned left toward freedom and the brilliant Orlando sunshine. Casey turned to the right, back to her dingy cell. I looked over my shoulder, and Casey gently waved before disappearing down the corridor.

We were mostly silent in the car. I felt that there were significant traumas in Casey's young life that needed to be explored. I explained to Jose that I needed time alone with the client to build the trust and rapport required to open up about sensitive issues. Jose agreed if it would get death off the table.

Most importantly, we needed to get a mental health expert involved as soon as possible. On this point, Jose appeared reluctant. I explained the critical need to coordinate guilt and penalty phase defenses. Jose agreed. I later found out that he already had brought in two state-appointed doctors to do an evaluation of Casey for a check cashing fraud case in which she was charged. From the death penalty point of view, a defense attorney never ever brought in the state's expert until you had your own private evaluation done.

After a quick lunch at one of Jose's favorite restaurants, we went back to Jose's office. Jose wrote me a check for the waiver package, and I settled in to review mounds of discovery until Casey's parents arrived. From the phone records, I noticed that Casey had been texting and talking on her phone almost nonstop in the days before her daughter was last seen. I admit that I was curious about this behavior, and had many questions to ask Casey's parents. Fortunately, George and Cindy arrived promptly and were quickly escorted into Jose's office.

Jose introduced me to them, and, as I had done with Casey, I explained the legal process to them. George asked most of the questions, while Cindy merely nodded her head. George sat next to me, and I had an opportunity to observe him closely as I explained the importance of personalizing — humanizing, if you will — a client in a death penalty proceeding. I sensed that he took everything as a personal failure on his part — a failure to lead and protect his family.

The blow to his self-esteem as a former police officer must have been devastating as well.

George seemed to grow increasingly despondent as we discussed the possibility of a death sentence for their daughter. George kept asking "Is this really necessary?" Cindy cried. In my experience, it is exceedingly difficult for families to accept the reality that someone they love might be convicted of murder and be executed. For this family, it was a double tragedy — the murder victim was their granddaughter, and the alleged murderer was their only daughter. In the end, they agreed to give me family pictures of Casey as a child and as a young girl to help with the waiver. I would get the photographs when I met them the next time.

I still needed to do an extensive forensic interview with the parents as well as Casey when I came back to Orlando. A forensic interview requires developing a rapport with a person. It takes time, and it is tricky to get someone to open up and tell you things that sometimes they didn't even know were lurking inside. A quick trip didn't allow enough time for thorough interviews. I was only there to lay the groundwork and needed to return to my practice in Miami for a few days. I would return in a couple of days to begin the interviews.

Part of the necessary groundwork was a meeting with the prosecutors. We needed to file a mitigation package with the state attorney. By doing so, we had an excellent chance of forestalling the filing of the state's intent to seek the death penalty. But first, we had to get the state to agree to wait for the mitigation package before filing its intent to seek the death penalty, or as it is morbidly known, the death notice.

In Florida, the state has 45 days from the date of arraignment to file its intent to seek the death penalty. Filing this death notice does not prevent the state from seeking the death penalty, but it provides the state with an advantage under the Rules of Criminal Procedure. The advantage is that if the state files such a notice, then the defense counsel must give notice of any mental health experts it plans to call during penalty phase and which mitigators the defense expects to establish through those experts.

When I returned to Orlando, Jose insisted on accompanying me to a meeting with the state attorneys. I waited in the courtyard for Jose to arrive, and we went to meet the prosecutors, Jeff Ashton and Linda Drane-Burdick. Once past reception, we were escorted to a conference room where Jeff and Linda were waiting. Almost immediately, I could sense the tension between Jose and the prosecutors. Both prosecutors were stiff and curt in their interactions with Jose. From the tone of Jose's questions and the prosecutors' abrupt answers, communication had clearly broken down between the sides.

Since it is up to the prosecution to waive the death penalty, I knew this tension and poor communication was not a good thing. Consequently, as death-qualified counsel, I did most of the talking and attempted to distance myself from Jose. Their attitudes visibly thawed toward me as I explained that my only interest was in the death penalty. I assured them that we would toll — not enforce — the 45-day limit under Florida Rules of Criminal Procedure if they gave us a couple of weeks to develop a waiver package. They agreed to give me time to finish the waiver before deciding to file a death notice. We courteously shook hands and left, Jose muttering derogatory comments once out of the prosecutors' earshot. Although I will never be sure, I suspect that this rift between the prosecution and Jose may have contributed to reinstatement of the death penalty months later.

Jose and I parted once outside, agreeing to meet for lunch. He had to attend to some business, and I had a meeting setup with the public defender. Because of the lack of defense funds, it was a very real possibility that Casey's case might end up with the public defender office. Additionally, the local public defender was an invaluable source of information regarding how the state attorneys pursued the death penalty in this jurisdiction. I wasn't disappointed when I met with Bob Wesley, the head of that office. A big, imposing man, Bob is known for his equally big generosity and commitment to the community and his job. He provided me with death penalty statistics and insights into the local personalities and procedures.

Armed with this intelligence, I briefed Jose over lunch on my meeting with Bob. After business was finished, I asked Jose how he had become involved in the case. Jose, although not practicing for long, had had a recent success by having a murder charge reduced to a manslaughter. The obviously happy client had been in jail with Casey when she was arrested for check cashing fraud and recommended Jose. The rest is, as they say, history.

I followed Jose back to his office to meet with George and Cindy again. This time George and Cindy did not appear as nervous. They had brought photographs of Casey for the waiver package. As each photograph was pulled out, George and Cindy became more engaged and animated as they described the memories surrounding each photo. "This one is from when Casey was born." "This is Casey and her brother." "Remember that Christmas?" A smiling Cindy and Casey posed for a special occasion in one; another was a family photo. Needless to say, there were tears at these remembrances.

George in particular was more engaged and asked numerous questions about the process and the waiver. When Cindy and George were finished with their questions, they left. I had the photographs that I needed for the waiver.

My next stop was the jail for an in-depth interview with Casey. Much to my surprise and irritation, Jose insisted on accompanying me to meet with Casey. There was little chance for the time and rapport-building I needed under the watchful eyes of Jose. However, I was still able to draw out a great deal of information about Casey's early life and pregnancy. Although I wasn't quite satisfied with the interview and felt there were many issues to be explored, I felt there was enough for a waiver, especially when combined with the photographs. Little did I realize that those photographs were the beginning of the end of the tenuous working relationship between Jose and me.

Additionally, my role as death counsel was not a secret for long. True to Jose's prediction, the media began calling me at my office on Monday after my first visit with Casey. Worse yet, I soon found my face and past clients sprayed all over the shows that regularly were following the case. I think that Jose became much more guarded after the attention I was receiving. This may have been the reason he refused to give me time alone with the client or the prosecutors as I had requested.

Back in Miami, Jose and I began telephone discussions on what would happen if Casey went to trial and was convicted. In death penalty cases, it is imperative that trial counsel and penalty counsel coordinate their theme of the case to the jury. The most challenging case is when trial counsel, at the insistence of the client, argues factual innocence and penalty counsel argues mental mitigation. If the guilt-phase defense is inconsistent with the penalty phase defense, the jury will not have a single theme upon which to base a life recommendation.

Jose and I had a series of discussions on coordinating the two phases. A rift developed as Jose wanted to act as lead counsel. Most disturbing to me was Jose's ignoring advice to begin developing mitigation. From my experience in other capital cases, I knew that it was important to find mitigation experts early on and begin developing a cohesive strategy.

Experts, good mitigation experts, are not cheap. Typically, I would hire forensic psychologists, psychiatrists, forensic social workers, neurologists, even cultural anthropologists, for the penalty phase, long before guilt phase even started. At this point, we needed more mitigation experts than we had — which was exactly none — and Jose did not appear interested in getting any.

However, I knew Jose's defense team might be under financial constraints. Knowing of these constraints, I still wanted the best for Casey and reached out to Dr. Xavier Amador. Dr. Amador had helped on one of my earlier cases, Yvette Yallico, the high school girl who heard voices commanding her to drown her baby. I was able to convince Dr. Amador to take on this case at a reduced rate. Even though Dr. Amador was willing to come on board, Jose continued to drag his feet and delay getting a mental health specialist. I was forced into preparing a major death penalty waiver package without the expert evaluations I felt were required.

Even as Jose's and my relationship deteriorated, my team was finishing the mitigation waiver package. By the time the package was ready to go, the communication with Jose had broken down completely. The conversations degenerated into terse emails and mostly silence. I focused on the job I had been hired to do — take care of my client and get the state to agree to waive the death penalty.

The Waiver

A waiver is designed to present the defendant as a human being, no matter how flawed or imperfect. It is important to remember that a waiver package is always presented as a hypothetical. The waiver package assumes that the client has been convicted of first degree murder and describes why the state should not seek the death penalty. The audience for a waiver is the prosecution, an audience that is already pro-death penalty. Because of this predisposition, a waiver is always presented in the light most favorable to the state. We typically use the state's theories of the case and attempt to show why these theories would ultimately fail in a death penalty prosecution. We try to show that even in the unlikely event that the evidence proves sufficient and reliable enough for a guilt finding, the evidence clearly does not support any of the statutory aggravators.

With Casey, the evidence had been released to the public through discovery. At this time, the primary evidence against our client was her behavior when the child was missing and the scant physical evidence, which consisted of hair and odor samples from the car trunk.

Filicide is Different

A wealth of information was available about Casey Anthony from published reports that showed her to be a good mother and a fairly normal young woman prior to Caylee's disappearance. The family was reported to be close and supportive, doting on the toddler. But the prosecutors still viewed this as a filicide — the killing of a child by a parent.

From my prior experience with Yvette Yallico, I understood that filicide is hard to fathom. Filicide has unique characteristics making it different from other forms of homicide. Filicide seems particularly horrifying and inexplicable, especially when the parent is the mother.

It's important to note that almost thirty countries outside the United States make a legal distinction between filicide and homicide because of the mitigating circumstances surrounding such killings. People around the world have recognized that filicide, sometimes referred to as infanticide, is a distinct form of homicide due to the impact of motherhood on women's mental status. The British Infanticide Act of 1922 provides that the maximum penalty in these cases is manslaughter, not murder.

But, this case was in Orlando, Florida, not Great Britain. Part of what I needed to do in the waiver package was to educate the Orlando prosecutors about this particular crime and the possible mitigation surrounding such an act if the case were to go to penalty phase.

From our research, we found that a general profile of mothers most at risk of committing filicide has developed. Typically, the mother is young, around 21 years of age. She is single and has had multiple unstable relationships with men. She might be a mentally deficient young woman or an apparently normal young woman, forced to put off high school graduation, college, or career because of pregnancy. She is unemployed and has financial difficulties. She may have suffered from serious mental illness in the past, or only manifested undiagnosed personality changes after the birth of her child. Roughly one fifth of these mothers have been victims of physical or sexual abuse.

Some mothers are classified as "denial mothers." Researchers talk about the "massive denial" of these women who kill their child. Typically, these mothers deny their pregnancy, often to the point where physical symptoms do not manifest until the actual "surprise" birth. The detached mother may deny the pregnancy out of resentment of the child, a lack of communication within her social network, or a fear of rejection by her family or friends. Interestingly, the families and support systems of these women do not notice the changes in the young woman.

Just as some families do not notice the pregnancy of denial mothers, the families of young women suffering from clinical or personality disorders often ignore "the elephant in the living room" and deny the problem. The result is that these young women are often at risk because they do not get the diagnosis, treatment, and help that they need due to unacknowledged or unrecognized mental disorders.

But a general understanding of filicide or a mental illness is not enough for a waiver. It is important to also show the weaknesses in the guilt phase evidence.

Attacking the Evidence

Death penalty trials involve more evidentiary hearings and challenges than other felony trials. This is especially true when a death penalty case relies wholly on circumstantial evidence. Where direct evidence, such as a body, a confession, or a witness is missing, the state bears an additional burden of proof. Besides proving the corpus delicti beyond a reasonable doubt, the circumstantial evidence "must not only be consistent with the defendant's guilt but it must also be inconsistent with any reasonable hypothesis of innocence." Thus, "it is the actual exclusion of the hypothesis of innocence which clothes circumstantial evidence with the force of proof sufficient to convict."

The reliability of the evidence is extremely critical in wholly circumstantial cases. The Supreme Court of Florida has not permitted factual issues to be resolved based on evidence that is not sufficiently reliable. Even fingerprints, the holy grail of comparison techniques, have been found unreliable in a federal court. In particular, many courts today are calling into question the reliability and value of expert testimony based on comparative techniques such as handwriting, tool mark analyses, and hair analysis. The Florida Supreme Court has agreed with a trial court that hair analysis comparison has limited probative value for its traditional use of identification.

The use of hair analysis for other purposes, such as determining postmortem intervals or postmortem shedding, is even more problematic than its traditional use of identification. The literature of studying the deteriorative effects of human head hair on forensic comparison is sparse; it consists of less than ten papers, only three of which deal with postmortem interval estimation. Of these studies, only two dealt with hair from bodies that were not buried under soil or submersed. The first study did not spend much time discussing the deterioration in this case, and the second and most recent reported study only used ten samples. The predominant conclusion seems to be that more studies are needed. A recent study found that where the postmortem interval is short before the hairs are studied, there was no significant difference between antemortem and postmortem hair samples.

In our case, the hair samples underwent two analyses: hair comparison and mitochondrial DNA testing. Only one hair was found that exhibited characteristics of apparent decomposition at the proximal or root end. The report did not indicate whether the basis for this conclusion was cuticle damage, yellow or dark banding, or fungal growth. None of the other samples from the trunk showed any evidence of decomposition.

One single hair, labeled Q12, was split in half, the other half, known as Q12.1, was submitted for mitochondrial DNA analysis. The results of the Q12.1 analysis indicate that the hair could have come from either Casey or Caylee, not surprisingly, as both used this car. No analysis was done to determine if Cindy Anthony could have been the source.

Another hair, labeled as Q46.2, was found on a shovel at the Anthony residence. Mitochondrial DNA analysis was done on this hair, which was destroyed during the analysis. Neither Casey nor Caylee could have been the source of this.

As to the odor analysis, first, cadaver dogs reportedly detected human decomposition at the Anthony home and in the trunk of the car. Second, two techniques were used to analyze air samples from the trunk: a comparison of the chemical signature of the air sample against a database and an analysis of inorganic elements in the air sample using laser induced breakdown spectroscopy ("LIBS").

Detection of human remains by cadaver dogs is problematic due to a lack of standardization in their training procedures as well as a "poor understanding of their scenting capabilities." Since 2002, the University of Tennessee's Anthropological Research Facility has been developing a Decompositional Odor Analysis (DOA) database. The purpose of the DOA database project is to help supplement cadaver dog training in detecting clandestine burial sites because the volatile compounds that dogs sense to detect live from dead subjects are unknown.

The DOA database identified over 478 compounds resulting from burial decomposition, of which 30 compounds that could be useful in training cadaver dogs. Of the 30 components, only 19 were found in surface decomposition.

Significantly, one of the results of this experiment was that "for the most part, human decompositional end-products are not very unique in the chemical world." Many of the compounds "can in fact be found in many outdoor samples taken virtually anywhere." Even though the concentrations of these chemicals were generally higher, "on occasion some control compounds showed elevated, transient concentration spikes for unknown reasons." Instruments used in odor analysis must be able to account for these concentration spikes.

In this case, the DOA database analysis of the air from the car was not conclusive because only a portion of the total odor signature in the trunk is consistent with a decomposition event that "could be" human. Only five compounds were significant to use for comparison. Significantly, fluorine compounds usually associated with human decomposition were not detected in the air sample from the trunk. The LIBS analysis of the air was "not conclusive."

Part of the discovery contained information about a large number of computer searches on the term "chloroform" and "an unusually large concentration of chloroform" in the trunk of the car. At the time, this information fed rampant speculation in the media as to whether chloroform was used to kill the presumably dead missing toddler. If the world in general knew this theory, we felt it was a safe bet that the prosecutors might have this theory. So, we had to attack the credibility of this as well. As to the chloroform odor in the trunk, one of the FBI forensic reports noted that the unusually large chloroform concentration "was far greater than what is typically seen in human decomposition." Even the investigators admitted the possibility that the odor signature was due to something other than human decomposition. During the trial, additional discovery showed that the computer searches turned out to be not so numerous and not so accurate.

Proportionality

From my meeting with the public defenders in Orlando, I knew that there were very few active death penalty cases in Orange County as compared to my home county of Miami-Dade. Prosecutors have the discretion to seek the death penalty, but each state attorney's office uses a different criteria. The criteria differs from jurisdiction to jurisdiction. What might be a death case in Orlando might not be a death case in Miami.

Because there are no state-wide standards, and as added insurance for Constitutionality, all death sentences in Florida need to be reviewed for proportionality. Proportionality review attempts to ensure that the death sentence really is appropriate in a case. As a result, the Supreme Court of Florida spends a large amount of its time essentially comparing the mitigating and aggravating circumstances of cases to be sure that the courts are fair and even-handed.

We needed to show that the death penalty in Casey's case was not proportional to other cases. For comparison purposes, we reviewed the nationally known cases of Andrea Yates and Susan Smith. Neither woman received a death sentence for killing not one but multiple children. In Andrea Yates' case, it only took 35 minutes of deliberation for the jury to choose a life sentence. Closer to home, we reviewed recent Orange County cases in which a parent killed a child. The prosecutors did not seek death in those cases.

As these cases illustrate, even if the state succeeds in getting a guilty verdict, juries often show mercy by avoiding the death penalty. Even though this country does not officially recognize that filicide is significantly different from other homicides, one U.S. study by respected researcher McKee found that local district attorneys prosecuted only 64% of 171 filicide cases over a 30-year period. Of those cases that are prosecuted, juries as well as prosecutors are aware of the mental and emotional mitigating factors that make the death penalty disproportionate and inappropriate in cases of filicide and infanticide.

After several weeks of work by my team, I packed the waiver in my briefcase and caught a flight to Orlando. I wanted to be sure that the waiver was delivered within the timeframe I had promised. The waiver was long, heavily footnoted, and comprehensive. Even though the package was quite detailed, it was carefully based on facts only publicly known. The reasons for waiving the death penalty were all out there. I just placed them into the proper context that, in the light most favorable to the state, would convince the prosecution to waive.

I had an ulterior motive in crafting the waiver from only public facts in case it became necessary to fight fire with fire—that is, if there needed to be some positive publicity about Casey. Prior to my involvement in the case, Jose had gone on the Nancy Grace television show in July to combat the negative publicity. He even had a public relations guy named Todd Black on the team.

However, Casey was already being tried in the court of public opinion and had become a villain in the eyes of many due to the mountains of publicity. I decided that a little publicity about the reasons that the state should not seek the death penalty could only help the client, as well as put pressure on the prosecutors to waive. I knew a member of the Orlando press whom I knew to be fair and trustworthy. I would use that court of public opinion to our advantage.

The Photographs

I am often asked how I can emotionally deal with cases that involve children. Some of the cases are horrible — dead children, sexually abused children, wounded children. As a father myself, I find these crimes unimaginable. Some attorneys simply disassociate mentally and emotionally from their clients; some plod through the motions; others don't last long in the business.

My solution? I see the clients as they were as children. Were they themselves subjected to horrible abuse, only to grow up and repeat that abuse? Did they even have a chance in the womb as their alcohol or crack-addicted mothers carried them? Did that blow to the head cause irreversible brain damage that prevented them from functioning normally? The image of the client as a child is a powerful motivator to me.

So, as we often do in waiver packages, we included the pictures of Casey as a child. The family had given these to me when I met them in Orlando. These pictures reflected a much happier time in Casey's life.

Jose had also received a copy of the waiver with the pictures. It wasn't until I received a threatening phone call from Todd Black that I was informed that the pictures in the waiver were on the market. Evidently, the defense team was trying to raise some much needed cash by offering exclusive rights to these pictures. Using the pictures in the waiver was a potential deal killer. My source in the media received a similar call regarding those pictures from Todd Black. A few months later, the news reported that Todd Black was a felon who spent time in prison for trying to extort money from a Los Angeles news anchor.

At this point, I was ready to end my involvement in the case. Jose and I were not communicating directly, and I did not want to be part of plans to hawk pictures of a client to the press. But, the state had not yet waived the death penalty.

Bittersweet Success

I emailed Jose a motion for a bill of particulars to file. This motion requests that the state identify the reasons, i.e., the aggravators, that they were going to use to support the death penalty. I hoped that this motion would force the prosecution to realize that Casey's case was not a death penalty case. Jose filed the motion on December 3.

The good news came on December 5, 2008. The prosecutors filed a notice that the death penalty was off the table.

My mission was accomplished. Death counsel was no longer needed. I immediately sent a letter to Casey and Jose withdrawing from the case.

After withdrawing and having so many disagreements with Jose, no one could have been more surprised than I was to hear Jose's voice when I picked up my phone a few days later. Jose thanked me for my work and understood why I was no longer on the case. He was calling to also ask whether the state, having waived the death penalty, could reinstate. The answer was yes, but at that point, I highly doubted this would become an issue. Unfortunately, I was wrong.

In the months after I left the case, a great deal of events transpired. Tragically, the little girl's skeletal remains were found. A blitzkrieg of news followed this discovery, demonizing my former client. In an effort to help from a distance, I went on Nancy Grace to reinforce the good judgment the state showed by its waiver and to show support for Casey and her defense team. Nancy Grace, while a passionate victims' advocate, is also a tough but fair interviewer — the perfect way to get the message out.

During this period, Jose and I seldom crossed paths. In early March 2009, I was teaching a continuing legal education seminar on the death penalty in Orlando. Andrea Lyons, whom I knew from her death penalty college out of Chicago, was also a speaker. I was a bit surprised to see Jose in the audience, because the Casey Anthony case was no longer a death penalty case.

Shortly after the seminar, Mike Walsh reached out to me again on behalf of Jose. He wanted to see if our differences could be worked out so that I might return to the case. I indicated that for my part, I would be willing to reconsider my decision to withdraw. Jose and I spoke briefly, I answered his questions, and sent him some of my background material.

The state filed a notice to seek the death penalty on April 13, 2009. Jose now had no death qualified attorney on the case. I began following the case again and was concerned at this turn of events.

Time passed. My concern grew as I heard no word that any qualified death counsel was on the defense team. My next move would further widen the gulf between Jose and me, but the client always comes first. I issued a press release stressing the need for a death penalty case to have a death penalty attorney. The state picked up on this and immediately decided to press the issue.

Soon thereafter, Jose announced that a well-respected capital defense attorney, Andrea Lyons, was joining the defense. I was pleased to see someone of her stature on the case. As a fellow capital defense attorney, I sent her an email with my thoughts on the case and insights into the workings of the defense team. Some of them were critical to Jose and his handling of the case. The email that I hoped would be confidential was not.

Soon after opening up to Andrea, I opened an envelope on my desk from the Florida Bar. The letter contained a bar complaint from an attorney that I had never heard of named Cheney Mason.

A bar complaint is the lawyer's equivalent of a nuclear strike. A complaint, if valid, could result in sanctions, and in the worst case, even ruin a career. Fortunately, the bar doesn't take complaints at face value and performs thorough investigations to see if the complaints have any merit. Most complaints never make it past the investigation stage.

Cheney Mason was filing the complaint on behalf of Jose Baez. Cheney related that Jose was upset with me for public comments I had made on the case without his permission. I was perplexed as to why one attorney would file a complaint on behalf of another attorney, especially an attorney that was quite capable of speaking for himself. In bar complaint investigations, attorneys can defend with details of the attorney client relationship. This includes financial dealings as well as case strategies and tactics. Both parties have to show their cards. By filing a complaint through another attorney, Jose avoided any personal or professional scrutiny.

Whatever the hidden motives, I took the complaint seriously and hired an attorney, Scott Srebnick, to deal with the bar investigation. As I expected, the investigation was quickly closed and the complaint withdrawn. For my part, I had spent thousands of dollars defending myself on a baseless accusation. I felt betrayed by Andrea Lyons. I was convinced that she had shared my private thoughts with Jose, although she didn't remember doing so. Worse yet, I was furious that a fellow attorney would be so vindictive.

It came as no surprise when Jose brought Cheney Mason on the team or that Andrea left the team. When the trial started, I feared that the death penalty might become a reality, but fortunately, again, I was wrong. In the end, the jury did their job.

Chapter Eight:
A Family Torn

PUNDITS OPINED THAT Grady Nelson was going
to die for the brutal stabbing death of his mentally handicapped wife and sexual molestation of his mentally handicapped 11-year-old stepdaughter. That was the consensus
among the top death penalty attorneys familiar with the case
of the 53-year-old social worker's aide, who had previously
been convicted of sexually battery of a minor. The only speculation was whether the sentence condemning him to
Florida's death row would be unanimous.

When David S. Markus and I were appointed to Grady
Nelson's case in 2005, we knew the odds were against our
client. We did not know that the case would take nearly 5
years, result in one mistrial, cost over $1.5 million in defense
expenses, and break new ground in admitting QEEG brain
mapping testimony.

The State's Case

The headlines of the Miami Herald proclaimed: "Rape, fear, murder destroy a family." Police responded to a disturbing scene at the Nelson family home on January 7, 2004. The police found Grady Nelson locked inside the home with blood spatters on his hands. Police looking through the front window and observed him hiding knives under sofa cushions.

Officers found a blood-soaked nightmare when they entered the modest two-bedroom home located in a poor but respectable Miami neighborhood. Grady Nelson's wife, Angelina Martinez — who neighbors described as a mentally retarded woman who loved to make doilies — had been stabbed 61 times. Her throat was slashed almost to the point of decapitation, and a butcher knife protruded from her head. Grady Nelson's 9-year-old mentally retarded stepson was hiding in the bathroom with multiple stab wounds on his upper body. His 11-year-old stepdaughter, also mentally retarded, was under the sheets of a bed, naked and bleeding from multiple stab wounds, which had caused her intestine to protrude from her body.

A Confession

Police hauled Grady Nelson outside, not sure whether he as a victim or a suspect. Within minutes, their opinion solidified: Grady Nelson was the alleged killer. They kept him manacled and shirtless in the grass outside the crime scene until they could summon a crime scene technician for a penile swab. Once at the station, Grady Nelson confessed to the murder and recounted the gruesome details to police officers. The confession was video-taped.

Rewind to December before the murders. That year, Grady welcomed the new year in jail. He was charged with sexual molestation of his stepdaughter. His wife went to the police and filed the charges that put him in custody. Angelina and her daughter were both mentally handicapped, even borderline clinically retarded. After failed attempts to get a sworn statement from them, prosecutors had no choice but to release Grady.

In January, a freshly released Grady came home to Angelina, his two stepchildren, and his five-year old son. According to his confession, the first thing Grady did upon homecoming was to have anal sex with his thirteen-year-old stepson, then anal, oral, and vaginal sex with his eleven-year-old stepdaughter. (Grady told the officers that the sex with the daughter had been regular since she was nine.) He then took the whole family out for a chicken dinner at a local Miami favorite, Pollo Tropical. Later that evening, Grady had sex with Angelina and her daughter with the stepson in the bedroom.

The next day, Grady found a letter from the Department of Children and Families addressed to his wife. Grady opened the letter and became convinced that Angelina was seeking evidence to prove the molestation charges.

His anger was fed by seeing a video camera in the bedroom. His paranoia exploded when he was told someone else was in the house. Grady was convinced that Angelina was spying on him with hidden cameras.

When the stepdaughter told Grady that someone was
molesting his five-year-old son, Grady became angry,
extremely angry, with Angelina. This was on top of a rumor
that Angelina was having an affair with a woman while Grady
was in jail. Grady stabbed her with a 10-inch knife from the
kitchen. He stabbed the children but he didn't want to kill
them.

Police responded to a 911 call from the house.

Picking a Jury

Collectively, a jury is smart, very smart. The jurors have an
uncanny sense of what the attorneys believe about the case.
They can smell our fears. The human reaction to fear is to
run in the opposite direction, to downplay the fear, to ignore
the elephant in the living room.

Picking a jury is an exercise in confronting your worst
fears and exposing them to the potential jurors, also known
as the venire. It requires an extensive and time-consuming
understanding of the pitfalls of a defense long before the trial
date. What will the venire think of our theory of the case
when confronted with the cold, hard facts?

A jury can sense our honesty just as well as our fears. For
me, the selection process begins with self-disclosure and honesty. I tell the venire what we are afraid of by front-loading
them with the worst facts of the case. Only by confronting
those facts can I have an honest conversation with the
potential jurors about their ability to be fair and impartial.

Part of the selection process involves death qualification
of the people who sit in judgment. A jury in a death penalty

case is different from your normal jury, aside from there being more jurors than a normal felony trial. The twelve jurors and two or more alternates cannot have a moral position for or against the death penalty that prevents them from following the law. And the law is considering both the aggravators and mitigators presented during penalty phase. They must be able to weigh them fairly and impartially before arriving at the appropriate sentence. Even if the aggravators outweigh the mitigators, the juror does not have to vote for death. That's the law, and they are instructed on it nowadays.

As defense attorneys, we need to find the killers lurking in the courtroom — the potential jurors who will not be open to mitigation, but only embrace the death penalty aggravators. These so-called moles attempt to get on a jury and get their chance to mete out their own personal brand of justice. The jurors who are morally opposed to the death penalty or have religious beliefs preventing them from sitting on the juror are usually quite vocal about their beliefs, but occasionally the prosecutors will ferret out an anti-death mole.

Both sides go to great lengths to find these stealth jurors. A juror in a death penalty case can expect a great deal of scrutiny. A background criminal record check is just the beginning. From the moment a person walks into the courtroom, we are observing them closely. Do they dress crisply or sloppily? Are they readers? If so, what are they reading? The potential leaders on the jury are identified. Which jurors cluster together during a break? Who smiles and nods when the prosecutor speaks? Who crosses their arms and looks away when the defense attorney gets up? Who stares at our client?

Back at our office, we have researchers pulling civil records, checking out property records, marriages, divorces. We find the jurors who tweet and the jurors who blog. We find out which charities they support, even their favorite sports.

This intelligence helps us focus on certain jurors to get them to open up and tell us their real feelings. The people who cannot follow the law, do not speak English (not uncommon in Miami), have severe financial constraints, or have medical problems are usually eliminated "for cause," which does not waste our precious peremptory strikes. Each side can excuse potential jurors for any reason by exercising a peremptory strike as long as that reason is constitutional. For cause challenges are unlimited and sometimes are heavily argued. I pitied the poor jurors who walked into Grady's case who had a vacation planned in the next four months — the judge wasn't buying that excuse.

Death Qualification

I was pleased to see that our judge was Judge Yvonne Colodny. An experienced judge, she was fair, and ran a tight, organized courtroom. This was her first death penalty trial, so I was comfortable that everything would be done by the book.

Fifty potential jurors were escorted into the largest courtroom in the Gerstein building on the first day of Grady Nelson's jury selection. The room almost reminds me of church — heavily wooded, high-ceilings, and solemn. Judge Colodny wisely borrowed the largest courtroom, which even

then was near-capacity with court staff, attorneys, and a panel
of fifty potential jurors.

Each member of the panel fills out a short questionnaire
before the bailiff brings them down from the jury room. Our
motion for a long comprehensive questionnaire had been
litigated and denied, so we were limited initially to the few
facts that the standard questionnaire provided. From the
beginning, I wanted to confront this panel with the negative
publicity about the murder of a mentally handicapped young
woman and the sexual assault of two children. We provided
the judge with a short summary of the news articles to read to
the jury after she read them the charges.

Judge Colodny announced the charges against our client
— first degree murder, two attempted murders, and aggravated child abuse on children under twelve. We were closely
watching the panel's reactions as the judge queried whether
anyone would have a problem being impartial just from
hearing the charges. Roughly a third of the panel raised their
hands without hesitation.

Pre-trial, we had won a very important motion that
allowed us to do individual voir dire — questioning — of
jurors. One by one, the jurors who raised their hands asked to
speak to the judge "in private," out of the hearing of the
other 49 members of the panel.

As each person came in, I think everyone was stunned
that the overwhelming number had either been molested as
children or had a family member who had been molested.
Some of these people broke down completely as they related
their own experience and had to be taken back to the cham-
bers to recover before returning to the jury pool upstairs for

reassignment to another case. As jury selection progressed through panel after panel, a request came from the jury pool room that we not send people back upstairs in tears — it was upsetting the people waiting to be assigned to panels on other cases.

We knew the aggravators that the prosecution would use. The heinous, atrocious, and cruel aggravator was foremost because the manner and method of the killing caused the victim a significant amount of pain, along with the sexual assault on the children. Additionally, the state theorized that the killing was a cold, calculated, and premeditated attempt at eliminating his wife as witness to his child abuse.

After nine capital jury selections, I was versed in the jury selection techniques of Cathy Bennet and Hirschhorn. Although I could not argue the facts of the case, I could ask questions in the form of hypotheticals to gauge a person's reaction.

I needed to find out who was open to our mitigation. Our client was a crack cocaine user. However, drug mitigation is a double-edged sword. Studies have shown that some people who will accept alcohol abuse as a mitigator will not consider drug addiction. We needed to find out who was open to considering brain damage as a mitigator. A QEEG (quantitative electroencephalograph) revealed brain damage from head injuries, drug use, and pre-natal alcohol exposure. These insults to the brain resulted in poor judgment and the inability to control impulses and rage. This evidence would be very important if we could get it admitted. But battling to admit the QEEG would be for naught if the jury wouldn't give it any credence.

Hypothetical after hypothetical concerning these issues,
as well as childhood trauma and race, were presented. The
initial fifty were whittled down to less than half a dozen
potential jurors. The next panel was brought in. After six
weeks and nearly 500 hundred jurors, the twelve jurors plus
two alternates were chosen. Trial was ready to begin.

A Costly Misstep

Nelson insisted that he was innocent of the crime and
demanded a defense of factual innocence. David argued factual innocence. With skillful deftness born of extensive preparation, he dismantled the damning DNA evidence and was
able to elicit testimony from an officer at the scene that
Nelson was impaired, incoherent, and appeared to be in a
daze. He also elicited evidence that Nelson burned videotapes
because he thought he was being spied upon by police, and
that there were empty cocaine baggies found in the house.
The elicitation of these facts supported the penalty phase
theme.

The trial ended in a mistrial in its eighth week because of
a misstep in direct examination of a key witness. Before the
trial, David Markus had won a motion that prevented the jury
from hearing during guilt phase about Grady Nelson's prior
conviction for sexual molestation of a child. During the testimony of the lead homicide detective, a reference to the
prior crime slipped out. A dead silence filled the courtroom
as prosecution, judge, defense, and the courtroom staff froze.
The silence was immediately followed by an objection. The

jury was escorted from the courtroom. The defense had to ask for a mistrial. The judge granted the request.

The jury was recalled, and Judge Colodny spoke directly to them. She explained that a mistrial had been granted and thanked them for their four months' of diligence. The jury was a bit stunned as they picked up their bags, their books, and their sweaters and filed out of the courtroom past the defense table. We stood as they walked past. To our surprise, several of the jurors nodded to our client. Two even shook his hand and wished him luck. As we left the courtroom, a very elegant, well-coiffed, matronly juror caught up with us and spit out "You all are pieces of shit." Overall, not a bad jury.

A mistrial is a hard decision to make. The harm to the case because of the wrongfully admitted information needed to be weighed against allowing the prosecution what was essentially a do-over. They now knew the weaknesses in their case. They wouldn't be caught by surprise a second time. In Grady's case, the knowledge of the earlier conviction for sexual molestation of a child was just too damaging not to risk a second trial.

The second trial was heard in front of a different circuit court judge, Judge Jacqueline Hogan-Scola. Another good judge — efficient, organized, and with a science background. The courtroom was much smaller this time — the administrative judge had loaned us the big courtroom last time and wanted it back.

We had different prosecutors as well. Abbe Rifkin was an experienced prosecutor who I have done battle with before. In the case of Harrel Braddy, a horrendous child

killing, things had gotten so contentious that we stopped
speaking. We eventually made up and left our conflict behind.
Abbe was extremely talented at connecting with victims. Her
direct of the victim of the prior sexual battery during penalty
phase had everyone in the courtroom crying — including me.
It was hard to cross the young fragile woman after Abbe did
her direct.

The other prosecutor was Hillah Mendez, also smart and
very likable. She was the brains behind the state's challenge to
QEEG, and knew more than I did. I had worked with her on
a few prior non-death homicides and she was someone I
could trust. I think she is one of the rising talents in their
office.

This time jury selection went quicker — it only took 2-
2.5 weeks and went through 200 jurors. Trial counsel's closing argument, which discussed reasons why the killing was
provoked by cocaine-induced rage, paranoia, and impaired
thinking, dovetailed with the penalty phase "broken brain"
theme.

The jury deliberated for nearly eleven hours before
returning a guilty verdict in Grady Nelson's wife's death. He
was found guilty of the sexual battery of his stepdaughter, but
not of his stepson. The jury returned guilty in two counts of
attempted premeditated murder for the stabbing of the stepchildren. The penalty phase battle was on.

Aggravators

The state was going to argue numerous aggravators in favor
of the death penalty. Prosecutors charged the prior violent

felony aggravator. A prior conviction for sexual battery on a neighbor's 9-year-old daughter supported this aggravator, and the now-adult sexual battery victim testified with devastating effect about how the rape ruined her life.

A second aggravator was that the capital felony was committed while the defendant was engaged in the sexual battery of a child or aggravated child abuse.

The third aggravator charged that the capital felony was committed to disrupt or hinder the lawful exercise of any governmental function or the enforcement of laws. The prosecution intended to show that Grady murdered his wife because of the sexual molestation of the stepchildren, and his fear that he would be arrested for the crime.

The state charged HAC as the fourth aggravator. HAC means that the capital felony was especially heinous, atrocious or cruel. "Heinous" means extremely wicked or shockingly evil. "Atrocious" means outrageously wicked and vile. "Cruel" means designed to inflict a high degree of pain with utter indifference to, or even enjoyment of, the suffering of others.

Additionally, the state charged the CCP aggravator because the state asserted that the homicide was committed in a cold, calculated, and premeditated manner, without any pretense of moral or legal justification.

The final aggravator reflected the mental retardation of Grady Nelson's wife, that the victim of the capital felony was particularly vulnerable due to disability.

Difficult Mitigation

The statutory mitigators seemed few in comparison. At best, the defense team hoped to convince the jury that Grady Nelson acted under the influence of extreme mental or emotional disturbance, and that he was so substantially impaired due to crack cocaine that he could not appreciate the criminality of his conduct or conform to the requirements of law.

But counsel is not limited to statutory mitigating factors; Grady Nelson's entire life history was used as a mitigating factor.

Initially, mitigation was difficult because Grady was not cooperating. The biggest problem is that people compartmentalize unpleasant things. Rapes, murder, and family secrets aren't easily shared, especially with an absolute stranger. Fortunately, our mitigation specialist, Cynthia O'Shea, was known for her tenacity and uncanny ability to unearth a person's life history, no matter how obscure or well-guarded.

For over two months, Cynthia worked to win Grady's trust. It wasn't easy. Grady would sometimes not bother to come to the interview room at the jail, leaving Cynthia waiting for hours. Cynthia quickly learned the hours that "The Young and The Restless" aired. This was Grady's favorite soap opera, and he would abruptly walk out on Cynthia when it was time for the show. Finally, she uncovered enough details of his life so that she could search for records and witnesses to document that life.

Investigating Grady Nelson's background for mitigating factors was difficult, due to his age and the lack of records. Grady Nelson grew up in a small rural Georgia town in the

1950s and 1960s. The town was segregated, and few records or accounts of the African-American community were kept. Older eyewitnesses had died, and any oral history of Grady Nelson's family life died with them. Cynthia was undaunted by the poor odds of documenting any of Grady Nelson's early life. She booked a flight to Atlanta — the closest airport to the still rural Hawkinsville, Georgia.

Traveling the roads from Atlanta was like traveling back in time. The red dirt, dust, and poverty still pervaded the town. The town, Cynthia soon found, was still separated by race. Her first stop was the town's funeral parlor on Main Street. In response to her query about Grady Nelson, she was directed to the other funeral home across town that "buried black folks."

She found her way across town to the funeral home/body shop. No joke here. Half the building was a funeral parlor; the other an automobile body shop. No one answered the door, so Cynthia wandered around the back of the autobody shop, where a middle-aged man was working on a car.

He looked up at Cynthia suspiciously in response to her question. "The funeral parlor? My mom runs it. Not so fast — first you're going to tell me who you are." Cynthia identified herself as an investigator trying to help someone who grew up in the area. Intrigued, the man wiped the grease off his hands and pulled out folding chairs, motioning for Cynthia join him at a card table. The story of her search for Grady's family unfolded over some of the best homemade pork rinds Cynthia ever had.

Better yet, Cynthia soon was inside the funeral home
talking to his mother. She showed the woman the death certificate for Grady's sister. The woman recognized her daddy's
signature, but Cynthia couldn't talk to him; he had died a few
months before. The funeral director's memories were vague
— she was only a young girl back when Grady's sister was
raped by three white men. The talk was that it was some
county fair workers who moved on. She remembered the
funeral and the odd detail that there was no autopsy. She
directed Cynthia to some other places.

Behind the funeral home were rows of little houses —
shanties really, no electricity, no air conditioning. People
remembered the stories of the little girl who had been raped,
but there were no records at the police station or the newspaper at the time. Finally, the town historian directed Cynthia
to a cousin who remembered the details of the young Grady
Nelson.

Grady's Life

Grady Nelson never knew his father. His mother was an
alcoholic prostitute who drank constantly, even while pregnant. There were no social service agencies available to the
African-American community, so when Grady's mother was
arrested, the sheriff would bring Grady to his mother's jail
cell, where he was fed and housed. Grady remembered that
he liked to sleep in the jail cell because it was warm and he
was fed good food.

At age four, Grady remembered seeing his sister being
raped by a gang of white carnival workers, while he hid

behind a wall, too terrified to speak. The sister died as a result of the rape, and Grady was left with a lifetime of guilt and recrimination. A death certificate was found for Grady's sister, but no details of her death were chronicled in medical reports, obituaries, or newspapers. Grady revealed that he had been abused as a young boy by a pastor, but there were no witnesses to the molestation, which was never reported.

Eventually, Grady's mother realized that she was an unfit mother and gave him to her sister to raise. Grady's mother abandoned the maternal relationship and Grady never saw her again. Grady rarely went to school, and began to experiment with drugs to medicate his personal pain. He was a very angry child, and began to get into legal trouble in high school. Eventually, to avoid jail, he enlisted in the military and continued to abuse drugs and alcohol. He received a general discharge as a result of his unresolved anger issues.

Grady reported being knocked unconscious several times and had a scar on his head. However, no military records or hospital records could be found to confirm these injuries.

As an adult, Grady became more dependent on cocaine and his life became less manageable. He had several drug-related arrests. He served a prison term. He was able to secure a job with the City of Miami as an outreach counselor helping to feed and shelter homeless people, but his drug use interfered with his job performance.

A Broken Brain

Despite the compelling circumstances of Grady Nelson's life history, the defense team felt that the jury needed to see

neurological evidence of a brain disorder that could explain
Grady Nelson's actions before they would be willing to look
beyond the facts of the crime — to listen to a mitigation case
and consider a life sentence.

A neuropsychological evaluation in capital cases should
be comprehensive because of the high incidence of
psychiatric and neurological disorders among murderers and
violent offenders. Research has demonstrated that brain dysfunction, especially in the frontal lobes, is a risk factor for
violence. Should neuropsychological or neurological disorders
be identified, the brain dysfunction and its association with
violent acts may be a significant mitigating factor in a jury's
deliberation.

The psychologists and neuropsychologists who examined
Grady Nelson found a clinical history of early childhood
abuse and possible closed head injuries. Objective testing was
needed to corroborate these findings because the history was
self-reported, and no supporting records existed.

Long before the trial began, I met regularly with my psychological mitigation experts, Dr. Rob Ouaou, a neuropsy-
chologist from nearby Naples, and Dr. Heather Holmes, a
psychologist on the defense team, who had experience with
QEEG brain mapping. Dr. Holmes suggested that a QEEG
examination be performed on Grady Nelson.

Quantitative electroencephalography, commonly known
as QEEG, is a child of the digital age resulting from the marriage of computer technology and traditional electroencephalography. A QEEG program amplifies and mathematically
transforms the EEG data. It then compares the data against
statistically-valid, normative databases of EEG data. A

normative database is a collection of brainwave patterns of individuals that meet certain criteria for "normalcy." The QEEG examination produces a three-dimensional, color-coded, topographical representation of the EEG waveforms generated by the brain. Utilizing a laptop computer, this brain map can be shown to the jury while the expert describes the findings and relates them to the behavior of the defendant.

QEEG is particularly well-suited for incarcerated or indigent clients. QEEG is inexpensive compared to other brain mapping technologies, such as magnetic resonance imaging (MRI) or single photon emission computed tomography (SPECT/CT) scans. MRI equipment averages over $1 million dollars, and SPECT/CT equipment averages around $1.8 million and requires a costly radioisotope for each scan. Because of the costs, the subject must go to a hospital or mobile clinic. QEEG equipment averages less than $10,000 and is portable. QEEG can be performed in any quiet room, which is easily arranged even in a jail or prison. Additionally, QEEG brain mapping does not require any prior patient preparation, which is important when the subject is incarcerated.

QEEG seemed to be a good fit for use in Grady Nelson's case. A well-respected local QEEG certified operator was recommended. The operator administered the QEEG using the FDA-approved Neuroguide™ system, developed by the prominent QEEG pioneer Dr. Robert Thatcher.

When the results came in, the QEEG brain map revealed frontal lobe brain damage consistent with Grady Nelson's predisposition to impulsiveness and violence. The results of the QEEG were highly consistent with brain wave activity found by other researchers to be associated with pre-natal alcohol exposure, loss of cognitive function consistent with traumatic brain injury, and early childhood abuse. These results were consistent with the Defendant's history. Now the only thing standing between the QEEG brain map results and the jury was the state's *Frye* challenge.

The Tipping Point

A court must prevent a jury from being confused by proponents of junk science. Accordingly, when the state raised a challenge to QEEG brain mapping in Grady Nelson's case, Judge Hogan-Scola ordered a *Frye* hearing.

Under *Frye* in Florida, an expert's opinion testimony that is based on scientific principles or theories is admissible only when the underlying bases are generally accepted in the field in which it belongs. The methodology applying the process must similarly be accepted in the relevant scientific community.

However, the *Frye* standard does not require the judge to assess the scientific reliability or validity of a principle or procedure. Rather, the only assessment required is to review the literature "merely to determine whether there is a quantitative and qualitative acceptance of the science." The judge is not required to become an expert, but only to determine "the level of agreement or dissension within [the relevant scientific community.]" In making this determination, a court may also consider scientific and legal literature, as well as other judicial decisions.

By the time of the *Frye* hearing, I had become not only extremely knowledgeable, but an advocate of this technology. I had spent countless hours reading volumes of literature that I also provided to the judge and the opposition.

The judge heard the testimony of Dr. Robert W. Thatcher, the nationally-known pioneer in QEEG analysis. Dr. Thatcher walked everyone through the technology, patiently answering all questions with clear and understandable explanations.

When the state called a neurologist as their star witness to opine on the unreliability of QEEG, I was ready. Essentially, a brain injury turf war exists in the medical community. Many neurologists, particularly the state's witness, believe that only medical doctors are qualified to diagnose brain trauma from an EEG. But this missed the point entirely — as Dr. Thatcher explained, a QEEG is not a diagnosis, but a diagnostic aide much like a blood test or x-ray.

As I asked questions on cross, the witness became increasingly hostile. He seemed irritated that he would be questioned. After discovering that his written papers on QEEG were less than a dozen pages in a book written years ago, and that he was conducting research using some of the QEEG technology he was discrediting, the judge abruptly interrupted my cross-examination. She had heard enough.

After hearing all the evidence, circuit court Judge Hogan-Scola admitted Grady Nelson's QEEG evidence. Judge Hogan-Scola found QEEG meets the legal prerequisites for reliability under Frye standards: "[E]verything I have heard, the methodologies are sound, the techniques are sound, the science is sound."

Penalty Phase Testimony

During penalty phase, the Grady Nelson jury heard about maternal abandonment, child abuse, child sexual abuse, and cocaine addiction, and seemed quite unimpressed. Numerous experts explained the mitigation to the jury. Dr. Marvin Dunn, a community psychologist, opined that Grady had maternal abandonment syndrome, a recognized DSM-IV syndrome, and explained the effect of childhood racism on his adult behavior. Dr. Heather Holmes presented significant events in his life as a "social historian." A psychologist who specialized in prison adjustment issues testified that based upon his review of prior prison records, Grady Nelson would be a manageable prisoner who was not a danger to prison staff. A psychologist with expertise in fetal alcohol syndrome and with the effect of cocaine on the brain's decision-making functions testified.

Even an oncologist described Grady Nelson's advanced prostate cancer and limited life expectancy. Unbelievably, although Grady Nelson was dying of cancer, the prosecutor wanted that cancer death to be while incarcerated on Florida's death row, not in another prison.

The impact of a color-coded, three dimensional, topographical brain map on the jury cannot be overstated. When Dr. Thatcher explained how the QEEG works in layman's terms and showed the jury the irrefutable evidence of frontal lobe damage on the brain map, the jury came alive. They leaned forward in their chairs and really studied the brain map. It was clear to the defense team that the jury now had a reason to vote for life.

After only one hour's deliberation, the jurors returned a recommendation of life for Grady Nelson. At least two of the jurors reported that the QEEG brain map evidence helped them make their decision for a life sentence.

Grady Nelson is appealing his sentence and maintains his innocence.

Conclusion

MY BROTHER AND sister attorneys will recognize these chapters as "war stories," things we share with each other over drinks or dinner. Every profession has them. Some may say that all I've done here is give you eight war stories, nothing more.

You now know that prosecutors believe the crimes I defend are heinous, atrocious, and cruel. On the other hand, many good people ardently believe that the death penalty is itself heinous, atrocious, and cruel.

I would suggest that in sharing my war stories with you, I'm giving you all I have to give. These cases not only provide examples of my past experience, they give you what I know: the human stories of lives gone wrong, lives that never really seemed to have a chance of veering off a path to destruction.

From these cases, I have learned forgiveness and mercy and compassion. I listen to the news differently now. I vote for education and food stamps and things that I know make a difference to people living on the edge. I know a little more about the answer to that question, *why?*

Maybe you will, too.

Further Reading

Cathy E. Bennett & Robert Hirschhorn, Bennett's Guide to Jury Selection & Trial Dynamics in Civil & Criminal Litigation: Cle Edition (April 1993).

K. Cauldwell, Living With Bipolar Disorder: One Woman's Journey Through Diagnosis, Understanding, and Acceptance.

James Hughes Collier, Estimating the Post Mortem Interval in Forensic Cases Through the Analysis of Human Head Hair (2005),
http://etd.lsu.edu/docs/available/etd-01242005-145140/unrestricted/Collier_thesis.pdf.

Linda Cylc, Classifications and Descriptions of Parents Who Commit Filicide,
http://www.publications.villanova.edu/Concept/2005/Filici de.pdf.

Duff, J, The Usefulness of Quantitative EEG (QEEG) and Neurotherapy in the Assessment and Treatment of Post-Concussion Syndrome, Clinical EEG and Neuroscience, 2004 Vol. 35 No. 4.

Frank H. Duffy, et al., Status of Quantitative EEG (QEEG) in Clinical Practice, at p. XVII, (1994), Clinical Electroencephalography.

F. H. Duffy, Topographic Mapping of Brain Electrical Activity: Clinical Applications and Issues, Topographical Brain Mapping of EEG and Evoked Potentials (1989).

Janet Ford, Note, Susan Smith and Other Homicidal Mothers-In Search of the Punishment That Fits the Crime, 3 Cardozo Women's L.J. 521 (1996).

John R. Huges, M.D., Ph.D. & E. Roy John, Ph.D, Conventional and Quantitativee Electroencephalography in Psychiatry, 199 (J. Neuropschiatry CLin NeuroSci 11:2, Spring 1999.

Leon-Carrion et al., A QEEG Index of Level of Functional Dependence for People Sustaining Acquired Brain Injury: The Seville Independence Index (SINDI), Brain Injury, January, 2008.

Geoffrey R. McKee, Why Mothers Kill, A Forensic Psychologist's Casebook (2006).

Geoffrey R. McKee & Stephen J. Shea, Maternal Filicide: A Cross-national Comparison, 54 J. Clinical Psychol. 679 (1998).

Cheryl L. Meyer & Michelle Oberman, Mothers Who Kill their Children (2001).

David Ovalle, A grotesque crime, a novel explanation, Miami Herald, 12/12/2010, Sec A, pg 20.

Larry S. Pozner & Roger J. Dodd, Cross-Examination: Science & Techniques (Matthew Bender & Company 2004).

Andrea J. Sedlak, David Finkelhor, Heather Hammer, and Dana J. Schultz, U.S. National Estimates of Missing Children: An Overview, in National Incidence Studies of Missing, Abducted, Runaway, and Thrownaway Children (Washington, DC: Office of Juvenile Justice and Delinquency Prevention, Office of Justice Programs, U.S. Department of Justice, October 2002).

Margaret G. Spinneli, Maternal Infanticide Associated With Mental Illness, 161 Am. J. Psychiatry 1548 (2004).

J. M. Taupin, Forensic hair morphology comparison – a dying art or junk science?, 44 Sci. & Just. (2005).

Thatcher, R.W. and John, E.R. Functional Neuroscience, Vol. 1: Foundations of Cognitive Processes (L. Erlbaum Assoc., N.J., 1977)

Thatcher, R.W., Hallet, M., Zeffiro, T., John, E.R. and Huerta, M., Editors. Functional Neuroimaging: Technical Foundations (Academic Press, New York, 1994).

Thatcher, R.W., Lyon, G.R., Rumsey, J. and Krasnegor, N. Editors. Developmental Neuroimaging: Mapping the Development of Brain and Behavior (Academic Press, Florida, 1996).

Arpad A. Vass, et. al., Odor Analysis of Decomposing Buried Human Remains, 53 J. Forensic Sci, 384 (2008).

Vass, et. al., Decompositional Odor Analysis Database, 49 J. Forensic Sci. 760 (2004).

David J. Yarwood, Child Homicide, Dewar Research, June 2004,
http://www.dewar4research.org.

Ron Word, Many Kids Die at the Hands of Family Members: Jealousy, Stress, and Frustration Can Turn Caregivers into Killers, Miami Herald, Nov. 8, 1998.

Kiel H.R. Wiedemann, The Pioneers of Pediatric Medicine – Hans Berger (1873-1941), Eur. J. Pediatr (1994) 153:705 (Springer-Verlag 1994).

www.ingramcontent.com/pod-product-compliance
Lightning Source LLC
Chambersburg PA
CBHW022038190326
41520CB00008B/626